INSIGHT I

UNDERSTANDING *Caravaggio* and his Art in Malta

ON THE OCCASION OF THE EXHIBITION

Caravaggio: L'Immagine del Divino

29 September - 30 November 2007

National Museum of Archaeology · National Museum of Fine Arts

SANDRO DEBONO

HERITAGE BOOKS
IN ASSOCIATION WITH
Heritage Malta
2007

Dedicated to my two angels
Katrina and Nikolai

Insight Heritage Guides: 16

Special issue to commemorate the 400th anniversary of Caravaggio in Malta

General Editor: Louis J. Scerri

Published by Heritage Books, a subsidiary of Midsea Books Ltd, Carmelites Street, Sta Venera SVR1724, Malta
sales@midseabooks.com

Insight Heritage Guides is a series of books intended to give an insight into aspects and sites of Malta's rich heritage, culture and traditions.

Produced by Mizzi Design & Graphic Services
Printed by Gutenberg Press

Photo Credits: Daniel Cilia, pp 24, 28, 29, 30, 31, 32, and 33; The St John's Co-Cathedral Foundation for the images of *The Beheading of St John the Baptist* and *St Jerome*; Heritage Malta and Heritage photo library. All rights reserved.

First published 2007

ISBN: 978-99932-7-164-2

Acknowledgements
This book would not have been written in a relatively short span of time had it not been for the unfaltering support of my colleagues at Heritage Malta. Special thanks to Dr Mario Tabone (Chairman) Dr Lucio Mule Stagno (CEO) and Heritage Malta top management for entrusting this project to the Arts Section. Special thanks also to Kenneth Gambin (Chief Curator) for reviewing all the texts and suggesting amendments and corrections, Antonio Espinosa Rodriguez (Consultant CEO) for enlightening discussions on some of its contents, Vita Secreto (Soprintendenza di Palermo) for indicating interesting references related to Caravaggio's Malta and Prof. Mario Buhagiar (University of Malta) for his support and suggestions. I'm also indebted to my colleague Dennis Vella for going through the text and discussing its contents, our volunteer at the Arts Section Dr Margit Waas for proofreading the text over and over again with much attention and Dennis Mema for his assistance in research. Our staff at Arts Section has also been very supportive; special thanks to Heritage Malta librarian Oliver Mamo and our summer student Stephanie Tanti for their patience and support. Last but certainly not least to my wife Cynthia and my family for their never ending support.

Sandro Debono
September 2007

Exhibition Credits:
Dr Albert Ganado
St Paul's Collegiate Parish Chapter, Wignacourt Museum, Rabat, Malta
Office of the Speaker, House of Representatives
National Library of Malta

With the collaboration of

GVERN TA' MALTA

SOPRINTENDENZA SPECIALE PER IL POLO MUSEALE ROMANO

with the active sponsorship of

and with the support of

CONTENTS

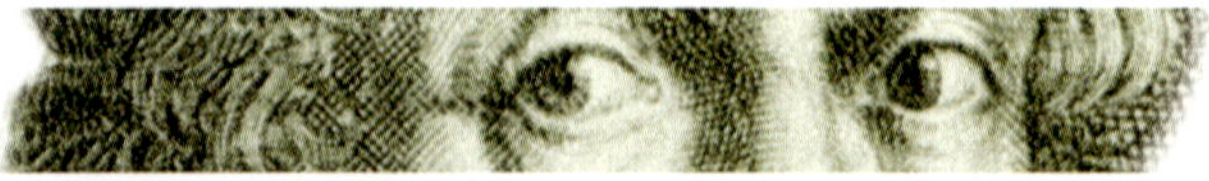

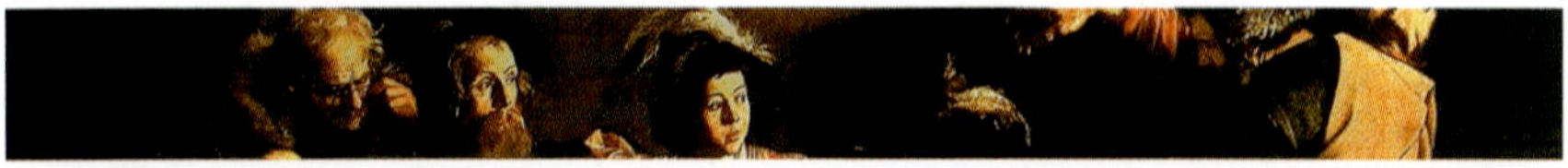

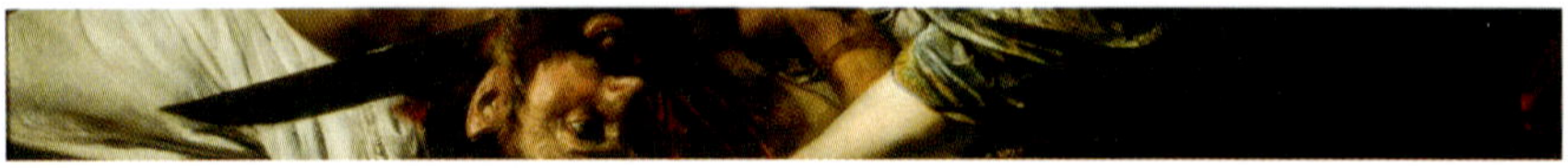

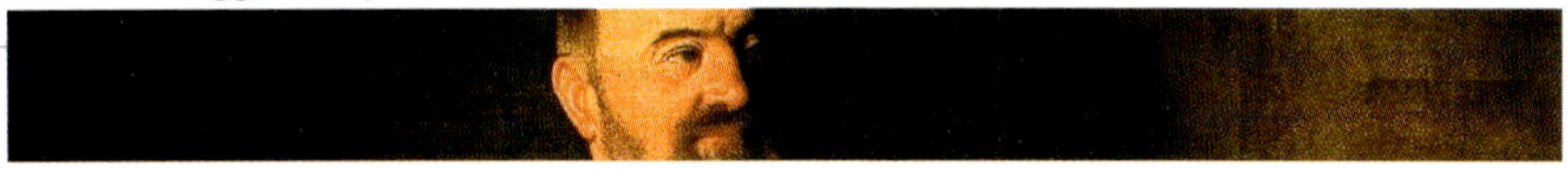

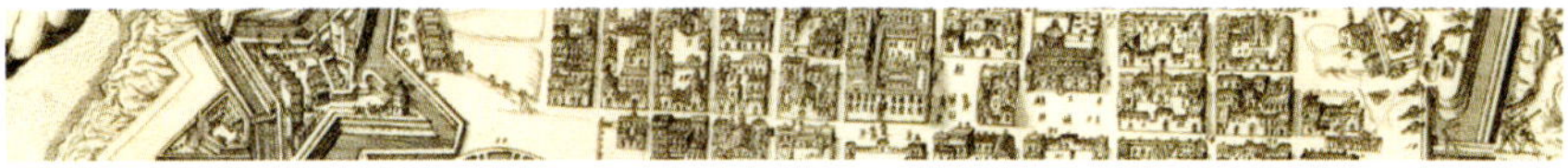

Cover: *St John the Baptist* (San Giovannino), Rome, Galleria Nazionale d'Arte Antica, Palazzo Corsini

FOREWORD

Caravaggio (1571-1610) is today one of the great icons in the history of western art. The notoriety of his short life, marked by uncouth and rebellious behaviour, but illuminated by bright flashes of creative genius together with the uncanny psychological appeal of his radically naturalistic paintings in which the sacred and the profane balance and compliment each other, have an irresistible fascination, that makes him an object of universal attraction. He epitomises an age of violence and religious intransigence with which the present day world can comfortably find parallels.

The *Beheading of St John*, that he painted for the Oratory of the Decollation at the Conventual Church of the Knights of St John in Valletta, is his largest and only signed canvas and, arguably, his greatest work. Shakespearian in its terse concentration on intense human tragedy told with superb visual economy that purges all inessential details and heightens its poignancy and dramatic effect, this is one of the most enduring masterpieces in the history of art.

Caravaggio's fortuitous stay on the island, four hundred years ago this year, has over the past few years, become a focus of art historical research. As Head of the Department of History of Art, at the University of Malta, I take pride in the fact that the Department through its Centre of Caravaggio Studies, co-ordinated by Dr Keith Sciberras, has been instrumental in clarifying some of the more nebulous aspects of the artist's Maltese experience, particularly the cause of his imprisonment and subsequent expulsion from the Order (cf. K.Sciberras "'Frater Michelangelus in tumultu': the cause of Caravaggio's imprisonment in Malta", *The Burlington Magazine* vol. CXLIV no. 1189 [April 2002], 229-231). The Centre, with the co-operation of the Caravaggio Foundation, has also been in the forefront of organising and sustaining seminars and lectures by leading Caravaggio scholars, and is currently in the process of setting up a specialised Caravaggio Library at the Malta University Library. The archival discoveries of Mgr John Azzopardi and the writings on Caravaggio's Malta by a team of acclaimed Maltese and international art historians, among them Dr David Stone, Dr John Gash and Dr Helen Langdon also deserve warm acknowledgement.

This book makes no pretence at academic scholarship. It is meant for the general public, but the author deserves credit for telling the story of the great artist and his Maltese context, in a factual straightforward manner that gives added meaning to the Caravaggio appeal for the non-specialist. Mr Debono is Senior Curator for the Arts with Heritage Malta and has the National Museum of Fine Arts under his direct responsibility. A postgraduate candidate in the Department of History of Art, he specialises in the Spanish-Maltese artistic relationship and has contributed handsomely to broadening our knowledge of this little tapped artistic link. His publications, that include a book on the art historical context of the Crucifix sculpture in Malta (*Imago Dei – Sculptured Images of the Crucifix in the Art of early modern Malta*, 2005), and his active participation in international history of art *fora*, have already earned him academic good repute, that his ongoing experience is bound to enhance.

Prof Mario Buhagiar
Head of the Department of History of Art,
Faculty of Arts, University of Malta

Map of the central Mediterranean area

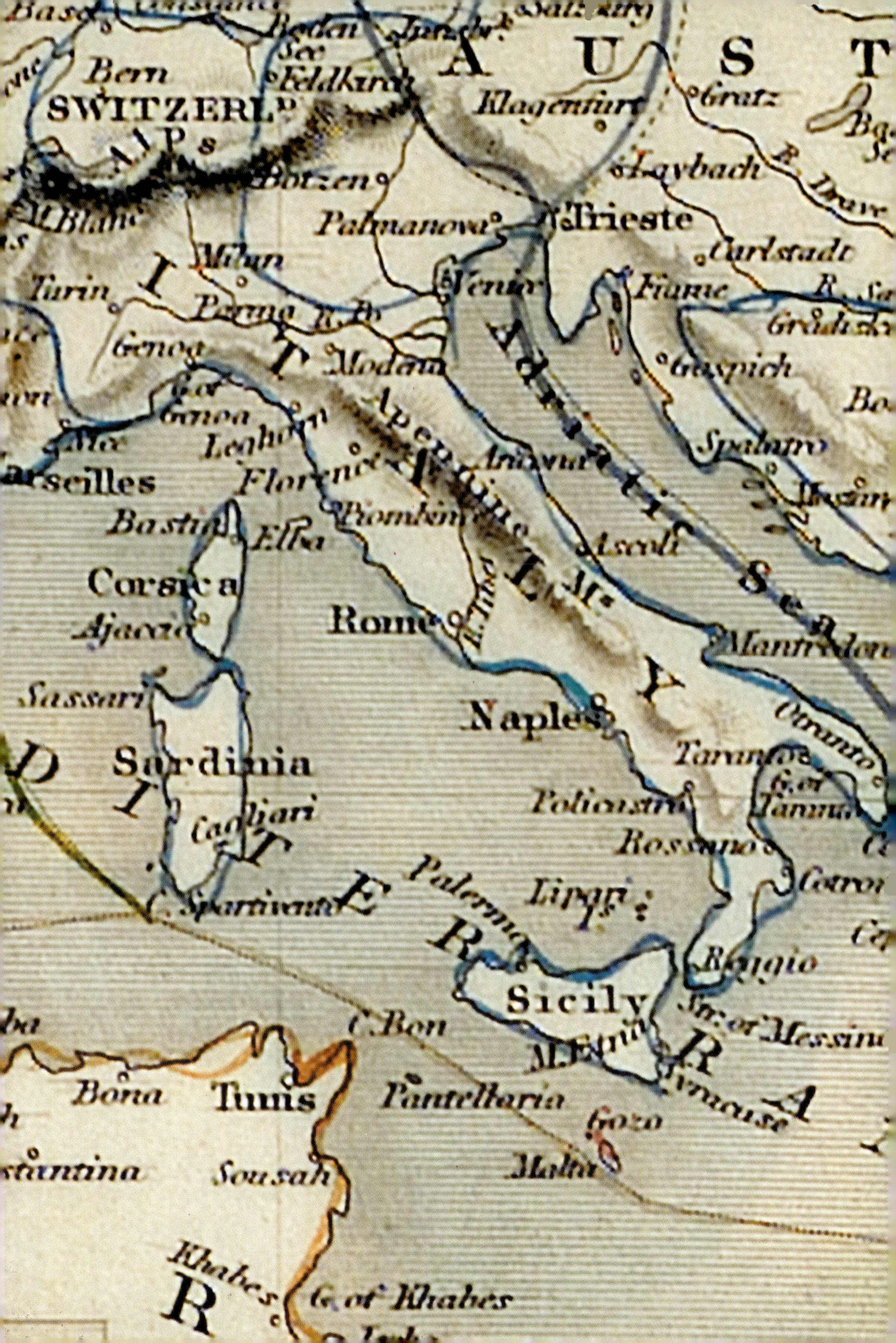
AUST
Bern
SWITZERL^D
Botzen
Klagenfurt
Gratz
Laybach
Trieste
Palmanova
Carlstadt
Milan
Turin
Venice
Fiume
Parma
Genoa
Modena
Gospich
G. of Genoa
Leghorn
Spalatro
Marseilles
Florence
Piombino
Bastia
Elba
Ascoli
Corsica
Ajaccio
Rome
Manfredonia
Sassari
Naples
Otranto
Sardinia
Taranto
Policastro
Cagliari
Rossano
Lipari Is.
Cotrone
Palermo
Reggio
Sicily
C. Bon
Str. of Messina
Bona
Tunis
Pantellaria
Syracuse
Gozo
Malta
Sousah
Khabes
G. of Khabes

Caravaggio in Malta - *timeline*

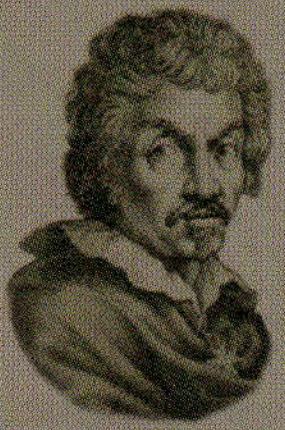

12 July
Caravaggio arrives in Malta on the galleys of the Order of St John captained by Fabrizio Sforza Colonna.

26 July
Caravaggio appears as a witness at the Inquisition Tribunal in an alleged case of bigamy.

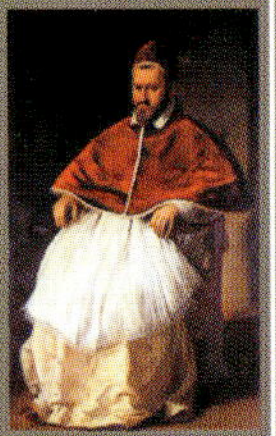

December 1607-January 1608
Formal petition by Grand Master Alof de Wignacourt to Pope Paul V asking for a one time dispensation to enrol as a Knight of Obedience 'a person of great virtues, honourable and respectful' who had committed murder but 'in order not to loose him'.

March
Caravaggio starts to work on his *Beheading of St John the Baptist* for the Oratory of the Conventual church of St John.

15 February
Pope Paul V accepts and grants permission to Grand Master Wignacourt to enrol Caravaggio within the Order

1607 June | July | August | September | October | November | December 1608 | January | February | March

Late 1607
Paints Wignacourt's portrait accompanied by a page (Louvre, Paris)

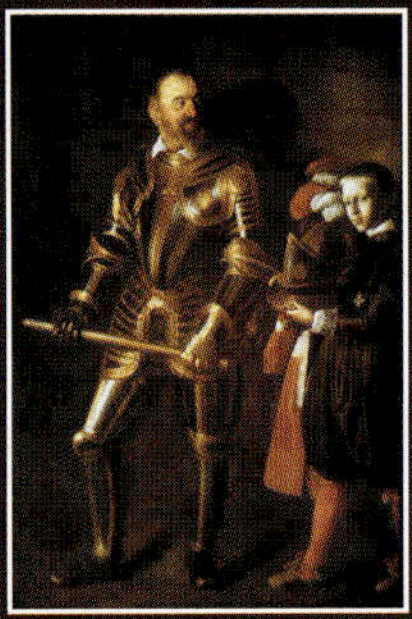

February 1608
Probably paints his *St Jerome* (St John's Co-Cathedral, Valletta) for the Knight Ippolito Malaspina who had travelled from Naples on the same galleys of the Order entering harbour the previous July

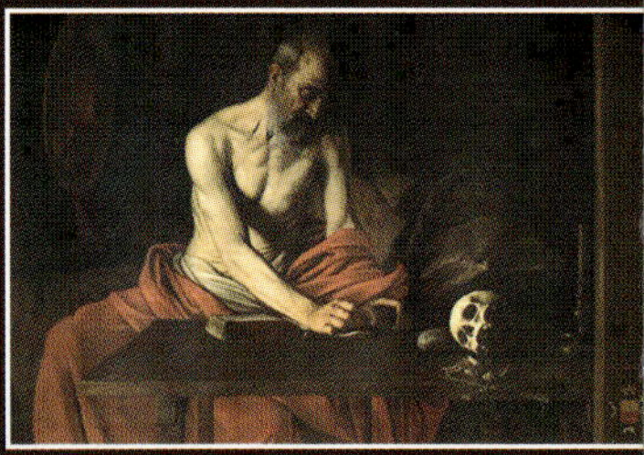

Source: Keith Sciberras & David M. Stone, 2006

14 July
Caravaggio is formally admitted into the Order as Knight of Obedience, one year and two days after his arrival.

18 August
Caravaggio is involved in a brawl with six other Italian knights in the house of the organist of the Conventual church of St John Fra Prospero Coppini in Valletta. One is seriously wounded.

19 August
A criminal commission is set up by the Order of St John to investigate the case.

27 August
The commission establishes Caravaggio's active involvement in the brawl. He is imprisoned in Fort St Angelo – a few days before *The Beheading of St John* was probably going to be unveiled

6 October
Caravaggio's escape from Fort St Angelo and from Malta (to Sicily) is officially reported to the Order's Council

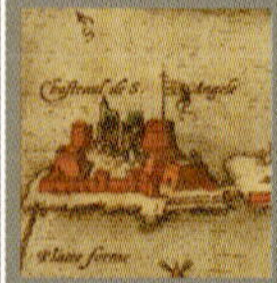

27 November
The Council hears the evidence of Caravaggio's escape and summons the Assembly to expel him from the Order

1 December
Caravaggio is expelled *in absentia* from the Order 'like a rotten and fetid limb'. The expulsion was held in the Oratory of the Conventual church in front of the painting which he had completed a short while before and signed as knight of the Order of St John.

April | May | June | July | August | September | October | November | December

May-August 1608
Caravaggio probably also paints his *Portrait of a Knight* identified as Fra Antonio Martelli (Palazzo Pitti, Florence) and his *Sleeping Cupid* (Palazzo Pitti, Florence) for the Florentine Knight Francesco dell'Antella.

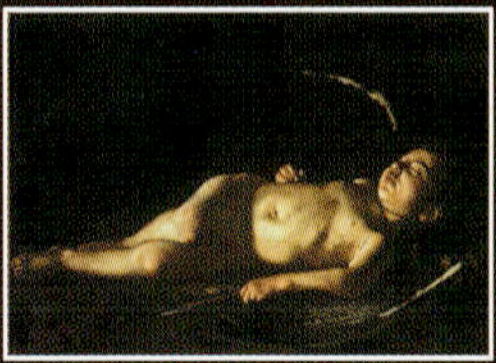

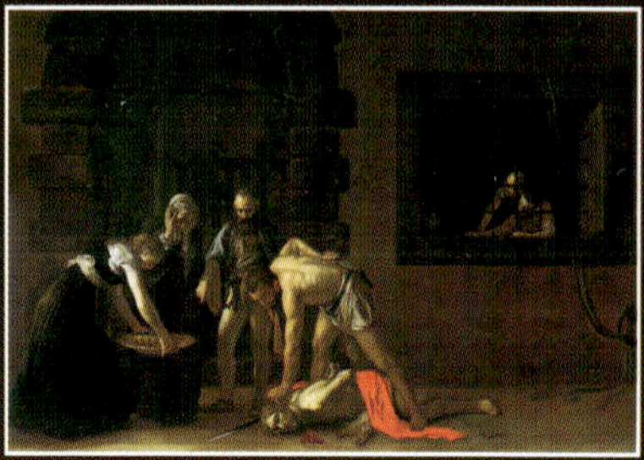

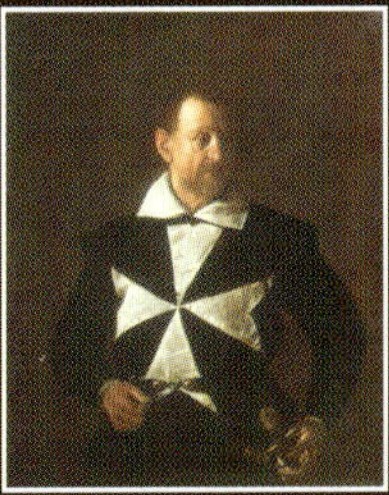

Late 1608
Scholars also suggest that Caravaggio's *Annunication* (Musée des Beaux-Arts, Nancy) was also painted in Malta during his last months on the island.

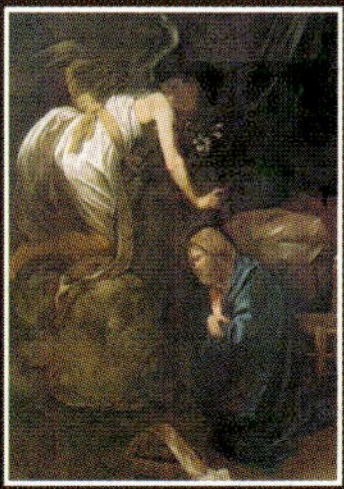

The Man called Caravaggio

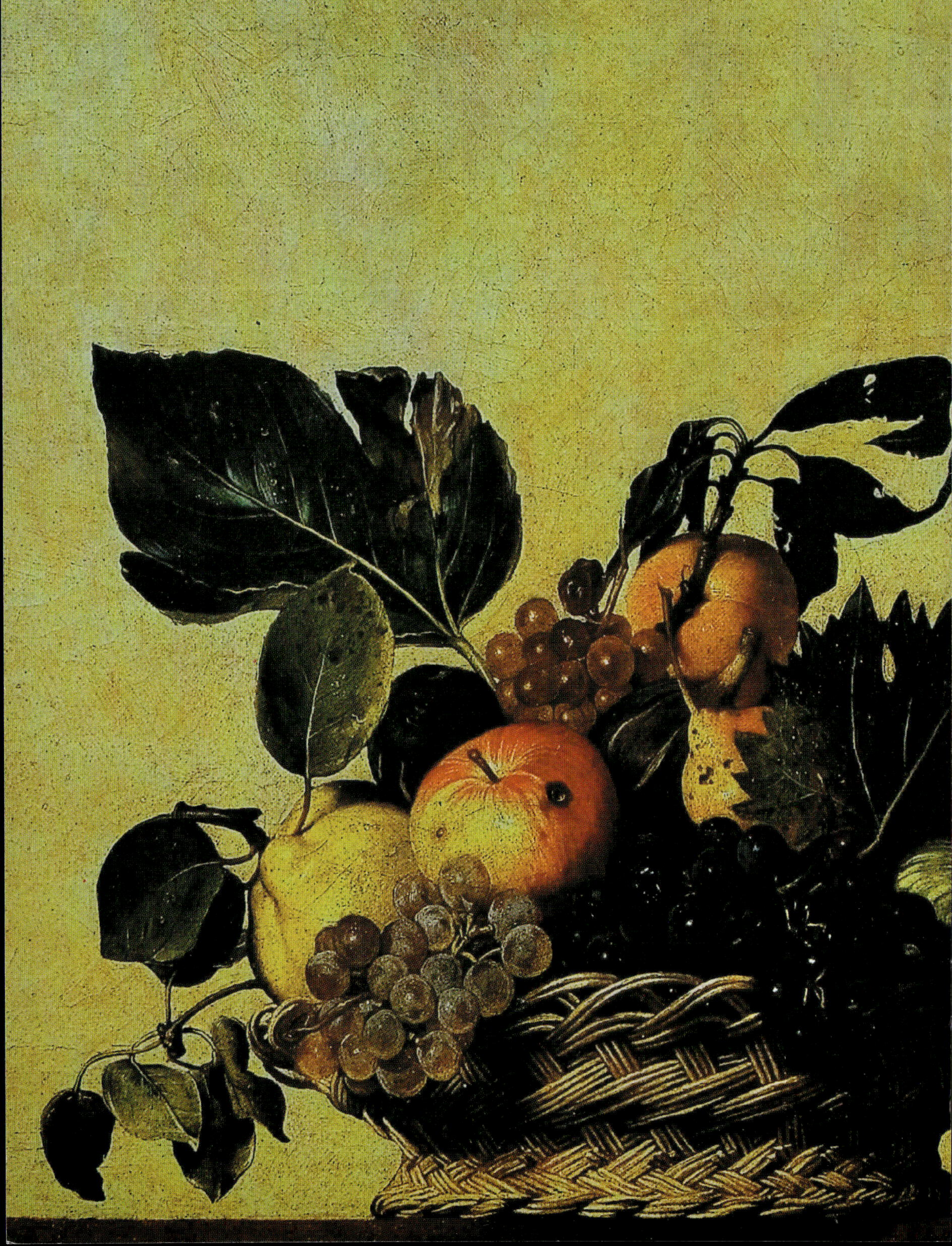

Michelangelo Merisi known as Caravaggio lived during times of great change in the socio-political setup of early modern Europe. Born in September 1571, Caravaggio was the eldest son of a middle-class provincial family in the services of the Marquis of Caravaggio; a town in the North of Italy close to Milan. His father, a widower with two daughters, had married Caravaggio's mother, Lucia Anatori in 1571.

The Council of Trent had come to an end eight years earlier in 1563; its decrees reinforcing the teachings of the Catholic Church on the sacraments and the cult of the saints. The Council also had upheld contested doctrine in the face of the inevitable scism between the Protestant north and the Southern Catholic Mediterranean. The situation was however far from resolved. The year following Caravaggio's birth, Catholics in Paris massacred thousands of Protestants in what became known in history as the Massacre of St Bartholomew. A few days after Caravaggio's birth, the Christian League gained an important victory over the Ottoman Turks at Lepanto. Although insignificant in military terms, victory at Lepanto brought about a feeling of relief. The Ottomans could however still wage war against Christian Europe and military campaigns and quests against them were deemed necessary.

Although Caravaggio was the town of the artist's childhood, the young man looked towards Milan for his artistic formation much like any aspiring artist of his time. Milan, then under Spanish rule, was a city of merchants, bankers and craftsmen mostly renowned for its armourers; its inhabitants were highly esteemed in swordsmanship and the art of the dagger. Milan was nonetheless a city of poverty that Caravaggio might

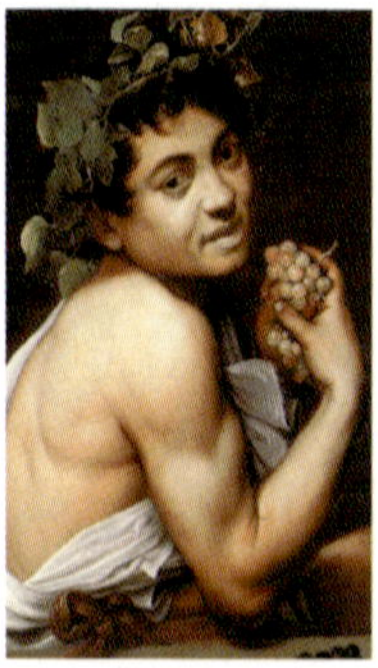

Caravaggio,
***Self-portrait as Bacchus*, Rome Galleria Borghese**

Caravaggio,
***Basket of Fruit*, Milan, Pinacoteca Ambrosiana**

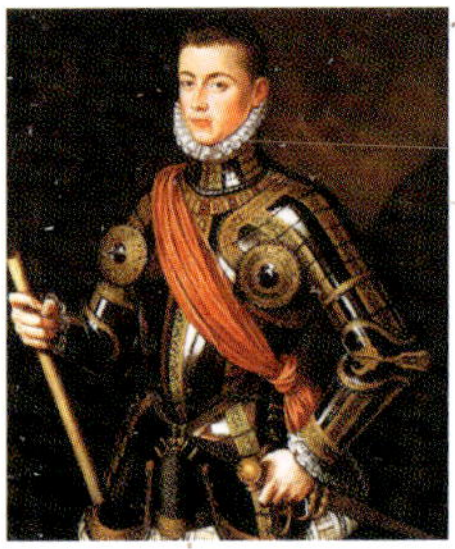 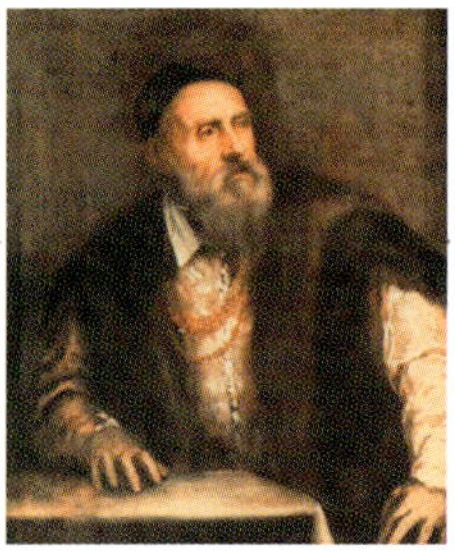 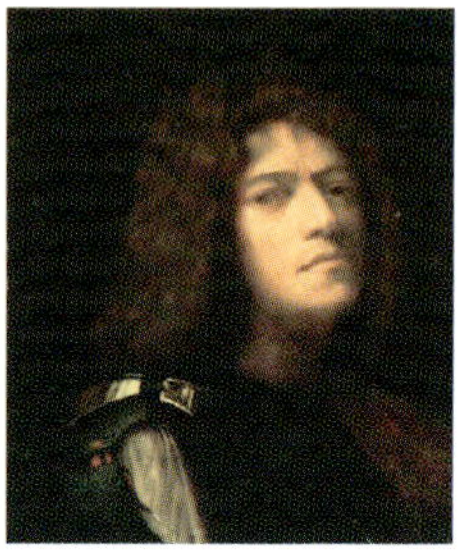 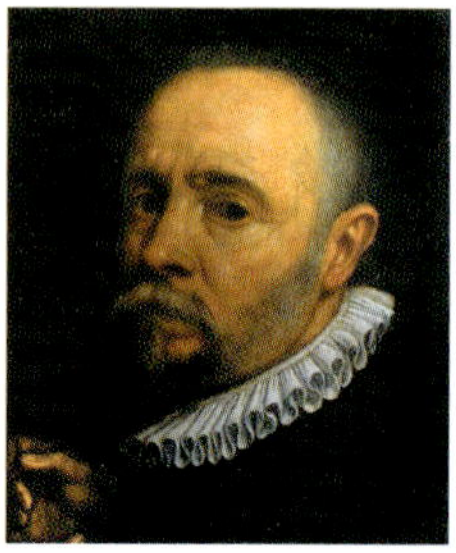

Above from left: Don John of Austria; *Self-portrait* by Titian; *Self-portrait* by Giorgione; *Self-portrait* by Simone Peterzano

have seen with his own eyes since young age. A year before his birth, the snow had driven many destitute from the countryside into the city of Milan. Many were to die of hunger. Poverty and bad social conditions proved fertile ground for illnesses to proliferate. The plague struck in Milan in 1576 and the young Caravaggio, then five years of age, suddenly lost both father and grandfather who were struck down by the plague within hours from each other. Milan had then prepared to host the hero of the battle of Lepanto Don John of Austria but the plague dispersed all the nobility out of the city and the expected cries of joy were replaced by suffering and misery. Caravaggio's mother was left a widow with small children to take care of.

Remaining in the then ravished city of Milan was the archbishop Carlo Borromeo; a saintly man and high ranking prelate of the Catholic church who had renounced the worldly splendour of a cardinal to live a simple and austere life. His zeal towards the poor and sick during the plague reaffirmed Catholic doctrine as discussed and approved during the Council of Trent where it was noted that salvation could be achieved through good works and devotion to Christ's sufferings in the passion. The poor acquired centrestage in Borromeo's preachings and became a symbol of the living earthly image of Christ.

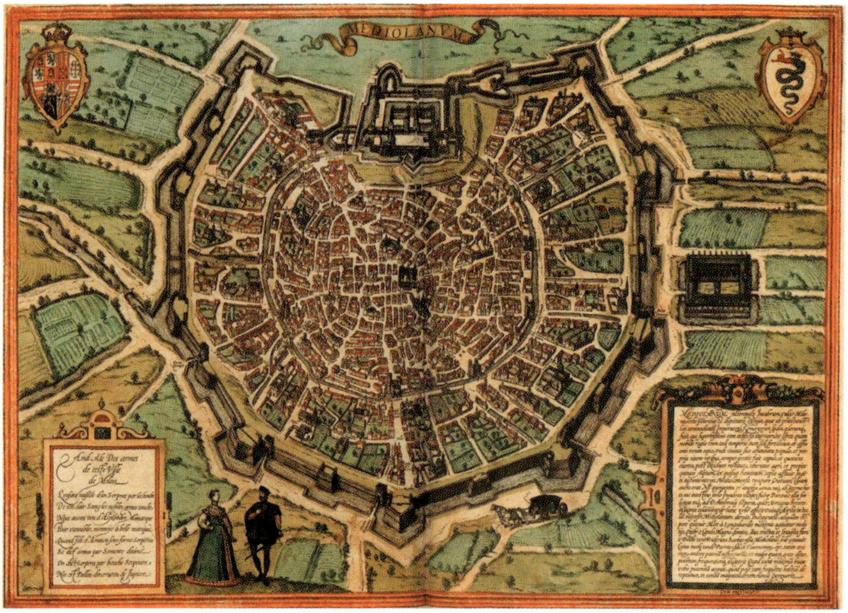

1572 map of Milan, (Braun and Hogenberg)

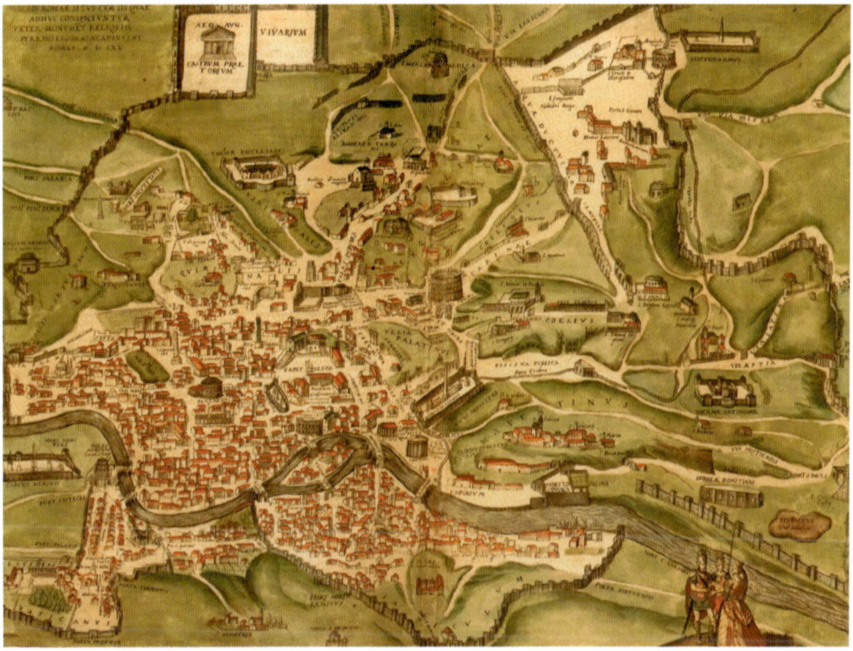

1575 map of Rome (Braun and Hogenberg)

In 1584, the 13-year-old Caravaggio signed an apprenticeship agreement for four years with the Milanese painter Simone Peterzano, an admirer and imitator of Venetian art. Caravaggio lived with Peterzano as was then current practice. In Peterzano's studio Caravaggio became acquainted with the rudiments of the art. He may have stayed on in Milan at the end of his apprenticeship perhaps expecting to win commissions from aspiring patrons through contacts that he had in Milan. But with the death of his mother in 1589, the young artist, then in his late teens, decided to sell his landed property acquired through inheritance and left shortly afterwards for Rome never to return to his hometown. The reason for such a hasty departure is shrouded in the mysteries of time; He might have killed a companion and had to flee quickly to Rome. His contemporaries do refer to his occasional outrageous behaviour as due to his hot nature and high spirits. Caravaggio may have travelled for a short time to Venice and Bologna where he could see and admire the works of Giorgione and Titian before proceeding to Rome.

Rome was then a small, bustling city that was gradually developing into a metropolis, yet still retaining a rural flair. It was above all else the centre of Catholic Europe and subject to the temporal and spiritual power of the papacy and dominated by powerful cardinals. Many lived in sumptuous palaces decorated with collections of note featuring art masterpieces. But underneath the crust of grandeur lay poverty and famine that created unsafe places. Bandits roamed the streets and assaults, mainly happening by night, were common. Street fights between the supporters of France and Spain, being the two main military powers of the day, were not uncommon. It was a dangerous and treacherous environment; large numbers of beggars roamed the streets and access to prostitutes was relatively easy. Some of these were supported by powerful local protectors administering areas of the city of Rome. The desperate situation of the poor and the homeless

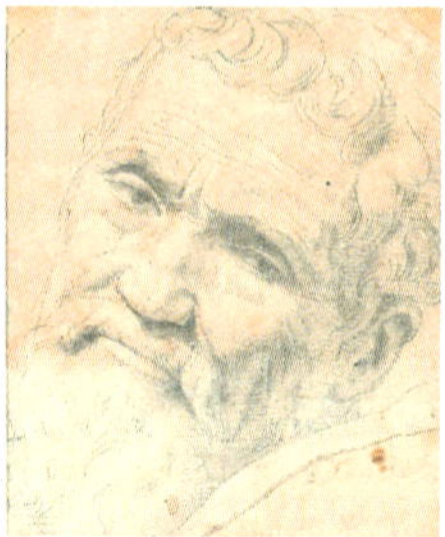

Above: Michelangelo Buonarroti
Below: Raphael

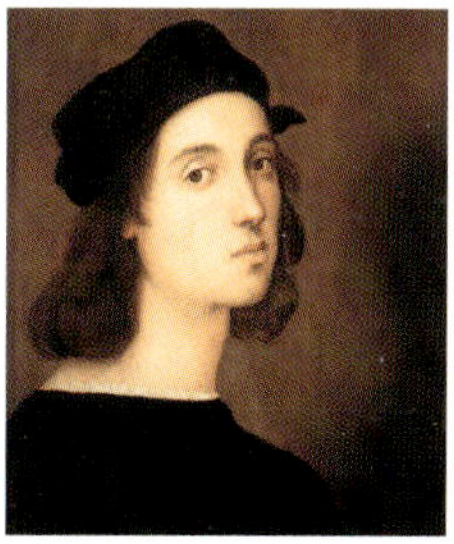

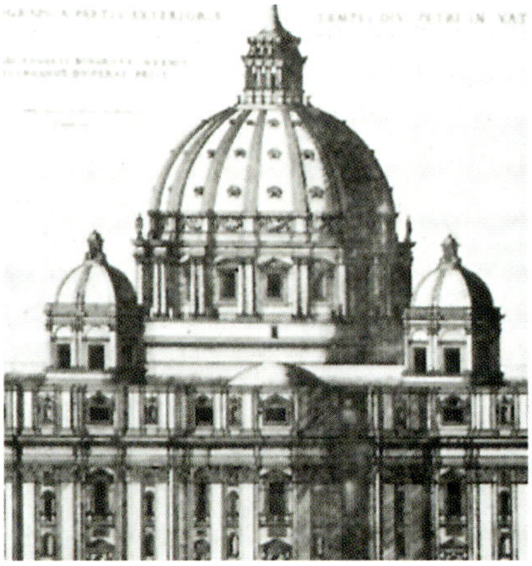

Michelangelo Buonarroti's dome for St Peter's, Rome

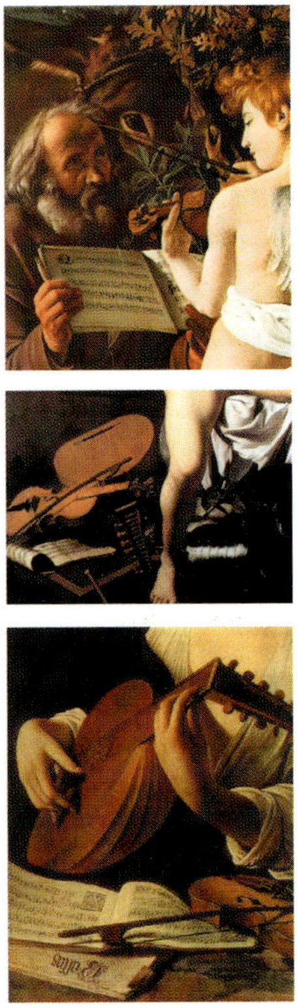

Details from Caravaggio's *Rest from the Flight to Egypt* (Rome, Galleria Doria Pamphili), *Victorious Cupid* (Berlin, Gemäldegalerie, Staatliche Museen), *Lute Player* (St Petersburg, Hermitage)

was slightly eased by the good deeds of the Jesuits of St Ignatius of Loyola and the Oratorians of St Philip Neri. It was believed that meekness of spirit could be achieved by moving closer to the poor and destitute. The fate of such a young and adventurous artist, like Caravaggio, could hold many surprises.

Caravaggio, an ambitious painter of twenty-one, was yet a stranger in such a busy city. Artists who visited Rome were mainly attracted by the great works of Michelangelo Buonarroti and Raphael which had been completed almost a century earlier; Michaelangelo's dome for the Vatican had just been completed a few months before Caravaggio's arrival in Rome and Raphael's art was a guiding inspiration for many. Artists were also after the study of ancient sculptures from classical antiquity that had survived in public areas and private collections. Many projects were underway or close to completion and art works were in demand. But what mattered greatly was the ability to enter the network of influential personalities and few could aspire to be appointed for prestigious commissions if not through these channels. Many painters from the North survived by selling run-of-the-mill paintings but to paint for the open market was no big deal and Italian artists would only turn to sell their paintings in the streets if in need of money. Caravaggio lived a harsh life carrying out odd jobs as a copyist or a painter of devotional images. He changed lodgings frequently and his behaviour suggests that he was not happy with the treatment meted out. His noble protectors from his home town could have intervened on his behalf to obtain a good and decent lodging with Pandolfo Pucci, the master of the household of Pope Pius V's sister. The services provided by Pucci proved below expectations to such an extent as to nickname the prelate *Monsignor Insalata*.

But Caravaggio's ambition spurred him on. From his first initial contacts with a little known Sicilian painter by the name of Lorenzo Siciliano, he moved to the studio of Anteveduto Grammatica, a cultured man with interests in poetry. This was just a brief interlude following from which Caravaggio managed to secure a job in the studio of one of the most fashionable Roman artists of the time. Giuseppe Cesari, known as *Il Cavalier d'Arpino*, was slightly older than Caravaggio and had come to Rome as a boy with his mother in extreme poverty. He had established himself as a fashionable fresco painter and cherished immense social ambitions. Caravaggio spent eight months with Cesari but his relation with the painter was indeed stormy. He was later to be taken ill to the hospital of Santa Maria Della Concezione. But the Caravaggio's works, so starkingly natural, were already proving to be incompatible with the classical idealisations of the times. Artists then looked upon Michaelangelo Buonarroti and Raphael for their source of inspiration yet Caravaggio's brush began to transform mythological and sacred subjects into real presences. He must have then lived with acquaintances or on his own but he later moved to the lodgings of a clergyman, Monsignor Fantino Petrignani who gave him a room in which to live. Caravaggio must have worked hard and would accept humiliatingly low prices for his works.

Towards autumn 1595, Caravaggio's art attracted the attention of Cardinal Francesco Maria del Monte, a Venetian cardinal with close allegiances and connections to the Medici family in Florence. Living in Palazzo Madama, del Monte had a personal interest in northern Italian culture. He was knowledgeable in music, theatre, the natural sciences and literature but most of all a patron of young artists like Caravaggio. But it is mostly Del Monte's circle of friends and acquaintances that were to prove decisive for Caravaggio's career. Palazzo Madama was very close to Palazzo Giustiniani, then the property of an up-and-coming aristocratic family that was later to patronise Caravaggio. Closely connected with this family was the Genoese Ottavio Costa; the most important Papal banker in the city who later also patronised Caravaggio's art. Other families who patronised Caravaggio included the Crescenzis who were later also to acquire works by Caravaggio.

Caravaggio's art begins to be gradually, yet steadily, valued within this circle of intellectuals and connoisseurs. Contemporary accounts describe him as a tall man with a thin beard, black eyes with bushy eyebrows and a mass of long, black hair over his forehead. He would dress in the finest materials and princely velvets but would only change from these suits when it had fallen into rags. He was described as a proud, satirical and quarrelsome person oftentimes behaving in a disorderly manner with an excessively fearless nature looking for the first opportunity to break his neck. He preferred black clothes; some would claim that his sinister appearance is reflected in his art. He spent his time in the taverns playing cards with his friends Lionello Spada and Mario Minniti but his band of fellows who rallied to the motto *nec spe nec metri* [without hope and fear] also included the painter Orazio Gentileschi and architect Onorio Longhi, another tempestuous character. Caravaggio's art absorbed him completely; he would paint tirelessly for weeks but then leave his projects and roam around with a sword at his side from one ball game to another.

It is through Caravaggio's connection with Cardinal Del Monte that in 1599, Caravaggio won his first large-scale historical painting for the chapel of the then defunct Cardinal Matteo

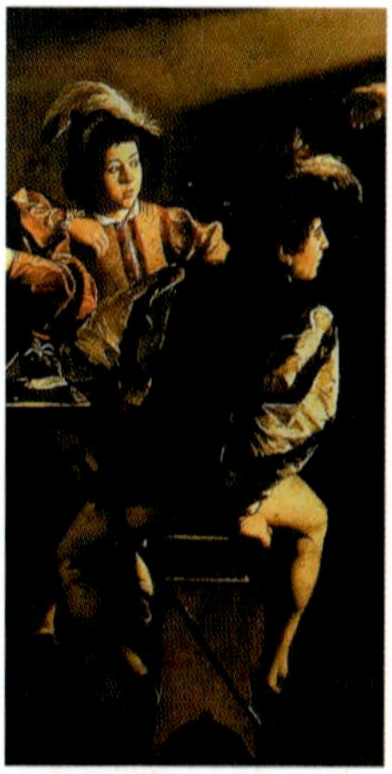

Caravaggio, *The Calling of Matthew*, Rome, San Luigi dei Francesi, detail

Below left: Caravaggio, *The Fortune Teller*, Paris, Louvre

Below right: Caravaggio, *The Cardsharps*, Fort Worth, Kimbell Art Museum

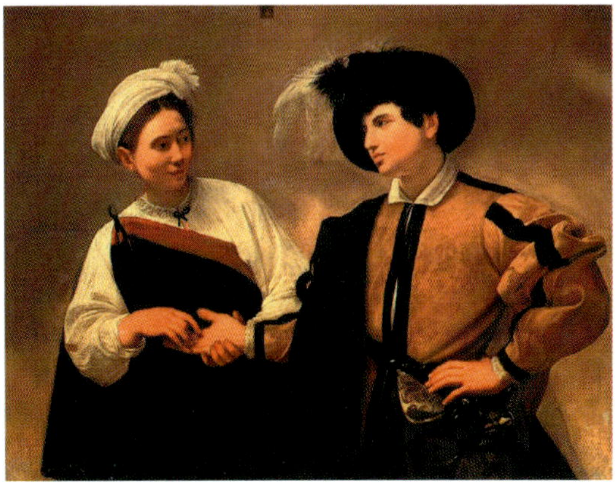

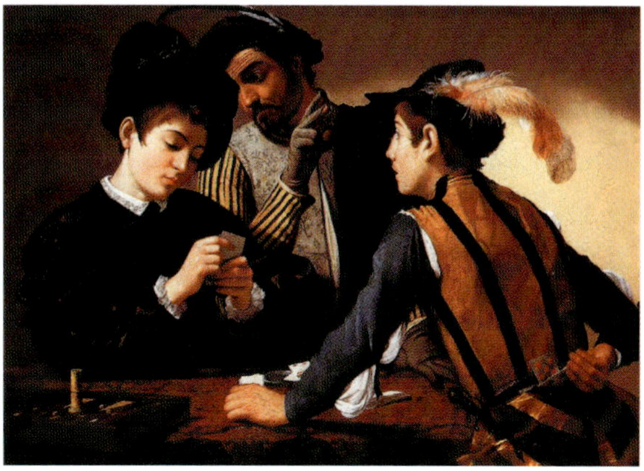

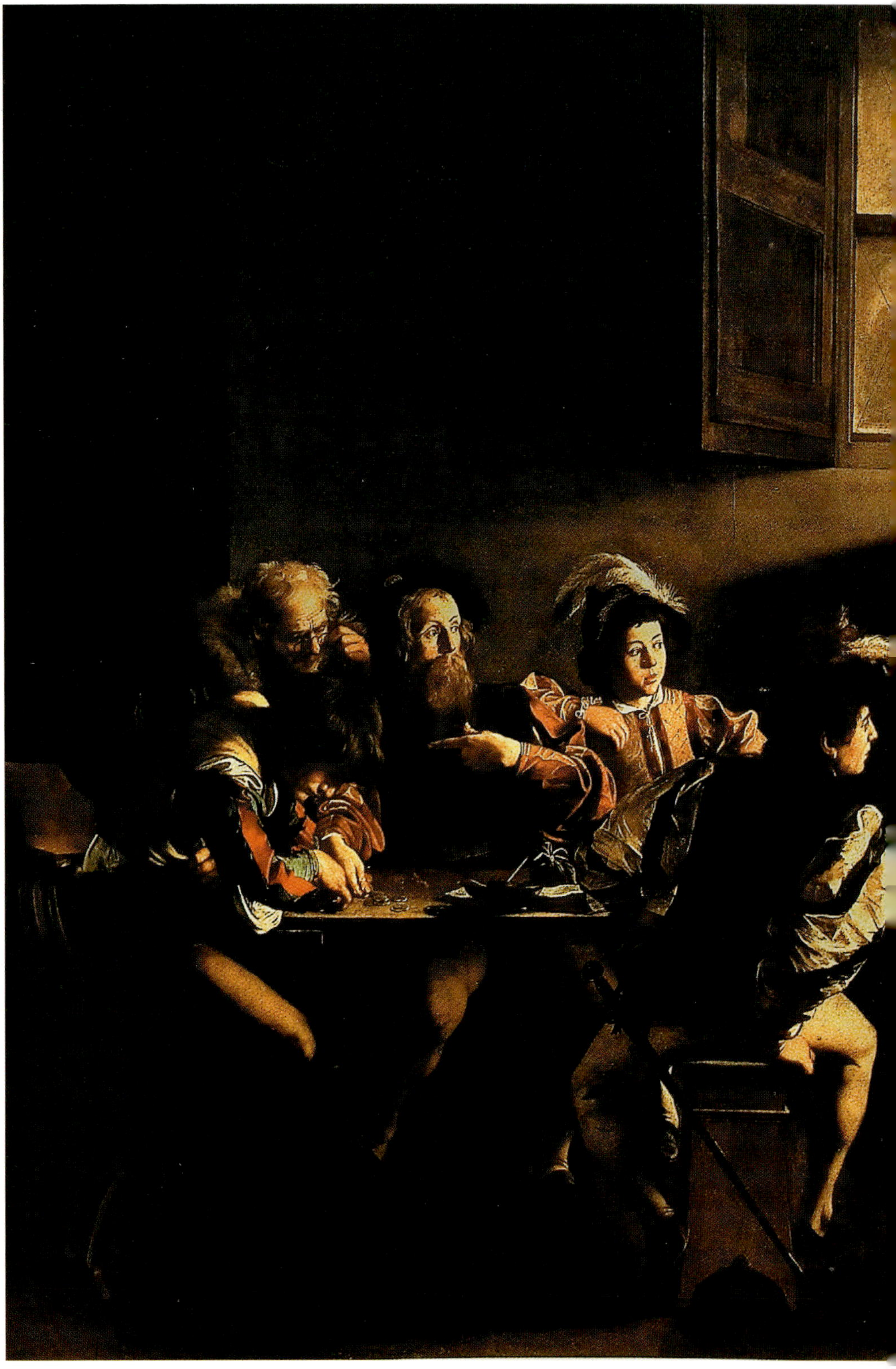

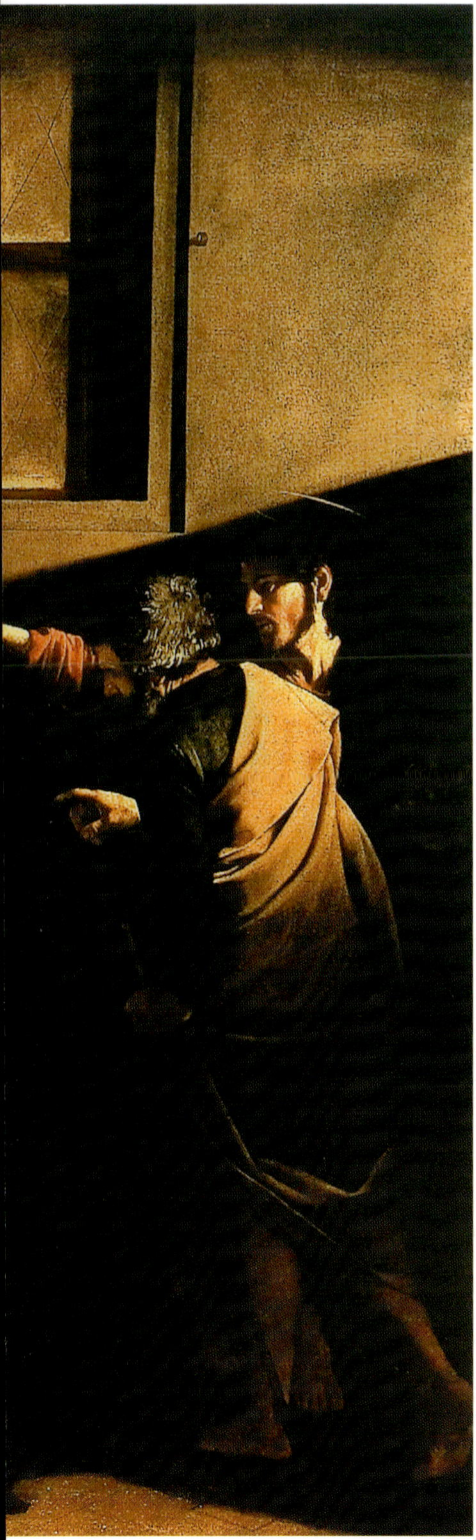

Contarelli in San Luigi dei Francesi. Thanks to this prestigious commission, the young Caravaggio now becomes the '*egregius in urbe pictor*' [famous painter of the town] whose art begins to rally young artists to follow if not imitate. Caravaggio is now a well-known artist fully aware of his achievements and celebrated within the artistic and intellectual circles of Rome and beyond. Yet he continued frequenting taverns by night from where he collected his raw material for his innovative and intriguing paintings. He despised many followers who tried to imitate him including his one-time employers who had by now become artistic rivals. Some ignored or scorned his works describing them as a mere reworking of Venetian art such as Giorgione's paintings which had earlier influenced Caravaggio. Worse still, some claimed that the popularity of his public works was not due to their innovative approach to nature but because they were sited near other, more known contemporaries. This criticism did not prevent such painters as Guido Reni from Bologna, then in Rome, from imitating him. Reni was an extremely pious man and greatly devout of the Virgin Mary. He

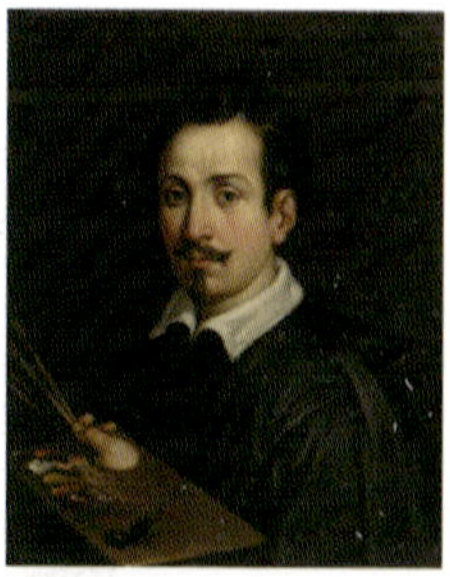

Guido Reni's self-portrait

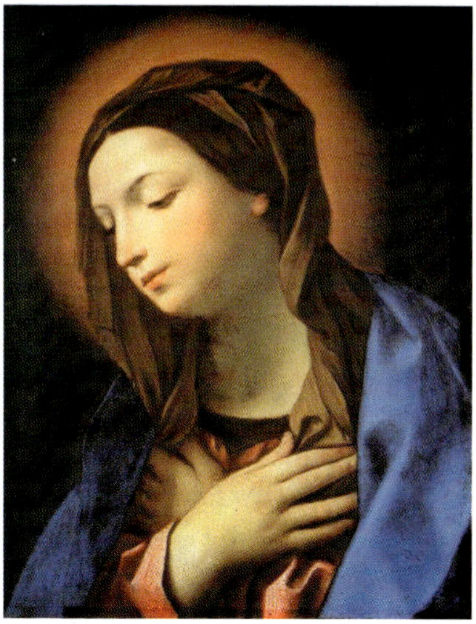

Guido Reni, *The Virgin of the Annunciation*, Germany, Landesmuseum, Oldenburg

Opposite: Caravaggio, *The Calling of Matthew*, Rome, San Luigi dei Francesi

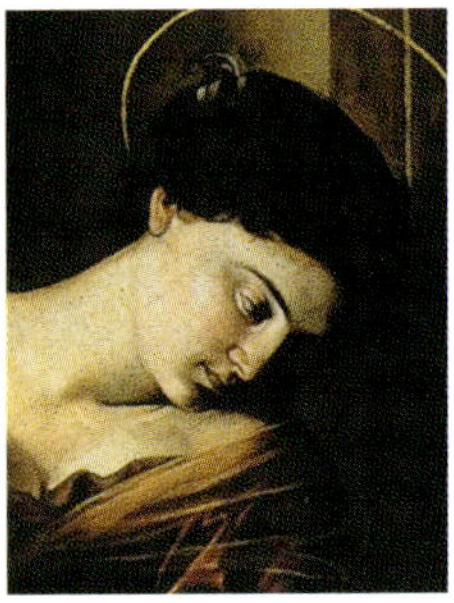

Caravaggio, *Madonna of Loreto*, Rome, Sant'Agostino, detail

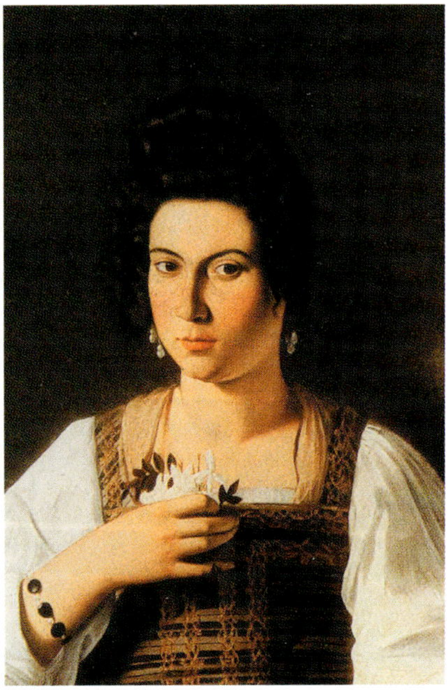

Caravaggio, *Portrait of the Courtesan Fillide*, formerly in Berlin, Kaiser Freidrich Museum

had studied with the Carracci brothers in Bologna. Many were to compare Caravaggio's works with those of the major exponent of the Carracci brothers, Annibale. Although the style of Caravaggio and Annibale Carracci is indeed different, their works have nonetheless many common points. Reni's *Crucifixion of Peter* is a reworking of Caravaggio's original composition for the Cerasi Chapel at Santa Maria del Popolo. Suspicion of foul play fell on Giuseppe Cesari, the Cavalier d'Arpino, who was accused of having lobbied for Reni to get this commission at the expense of Caravaggio.

Caravaggio, *The Taking of Christ*, Dublin, National Gallery

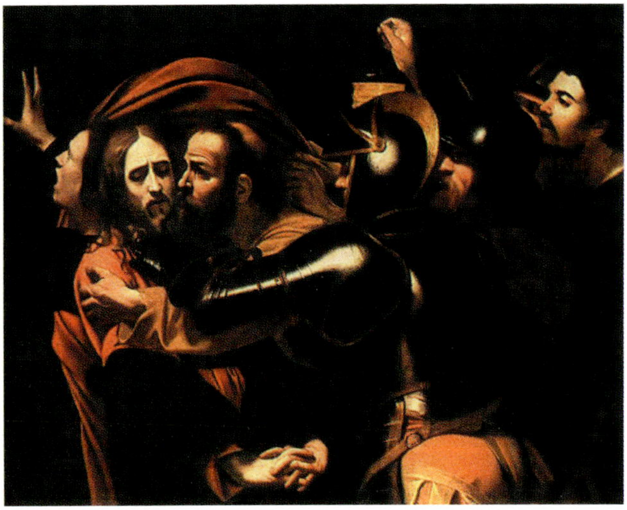

In such circumstances, Caravaggio did not fail to hit back with equal scorn. Giovanni Baglione, a painter who imitated Caravaggio's style, accused him and his circle of friends of distributing malicious and slanderous poems written against him in foul and obscene language. Baglione accused Caravaggio and his circle of friends of acting out of envy but the court proceedings instituted by Baglione against them confirm Caravaggio's poor opinion of Baglione. Caravaggio considered not to be worthy of his high self-expectations boosted by the coveted golden chain that he carried around his neck granted to artists by patrons for their virtuosity. Caravaggio's spate of revenge did not limit itself to his art and his quick-handed reaction brought him into trouble more than ever as in previous occasions. He affronted Messer Girolamo Stampa de Montepulciano, from the household of his protector Cardinal del Monte, with a club and threatened him with a sword. Caravaggio also challenged his one-time employer Giuseppe Cesari, the Cavalier d'Arpino, to a duel but the latter rebuked his challenge as unworthy of consideration. Caravaggio is arrested for carrying weapons at night without a license but rebukes this arrest by affirming that he was in the services of a cardinal or that he had verbal approval from the Governor of Rome, who had given orders to the captain and his corporal to let him carry arms.

Caravaggio's spate of violence continues even after he leaves the del Monte's household moving on to that of Cardinal Girolamo Mattei in 1601. A friend of the Giustinianis, the Matteis were also close to Cardinal Del Monte and like the Giustinianis and del Monte, they fostered an interest in the arts not least in Caravaggio's paintings which they were also to acquire. A tavernkeeper at the Osteria del Moro accused Caravaggio of throwing a plate with artichokes at his face and wounding his left cheek while threatening him with his sword. Caravaggio is frequently imprisoned for such mishaps as insulting the Roman police whom he occasionally also pelts and assaults. His sword and dagger are confiscated and he reacts violently to anything that he perceives as wrong. He threw stones at the house of a landlady in Campo Marzio for confiscating his goods after not paying the due rent. Brawls often leave him injured. In one instance he is wounded on his left ear and throat but, on being questioned by the local magistrate, Caravaggio claimed that the wounds were self-inflicted. None who spoke against him or tried to spite him would get away with it. A young notary named Mariano Pasqualone spread defamatory accusations against him concerning a young woman named Lena who acted as his model. Caravaggio assaulted him after nightfall striking Pasqualone with a sword on the head and then ran away into the dark. He had to flee to Genoa and could only return to Rome on condition that he apologised to Pasqualone for his deeds to receive an official pardon.

By 1605 Caravaggio was living on his own with very little comfort; his possessions then included an odd array of cutlery and crockery, minimal furnishings and a few clothes, mostly torn. Caravaggio had by now also suffered more than one rejection of his public paintings. His *St Matthew*, painted as an illiterate commoner stressing his seemingly scarce intellect to write his gospel, had been rejected on grounds of sheer lack of decorum. This was not the right way to present one of the four chroniclers of the life of Christ to the faithful of his time. His *Death of the Virgin* imitating the mortal death of a young lady dressed in red and his Virgin holding the naked Christ child whilst trampling over a coiled serpent also suffered the same fate.

Matters came to a head on the evening of 28th May 1606. Caravaggio and his gang engaged in a violent and bloody street fight with Ranuccio Tommasoni, a tough guy and protégé of the powerful Farnese family. The argument apparently started over a game of *pallacorda* – what is tennis today – but both had previously crossed swords over women. The duel went on for hours

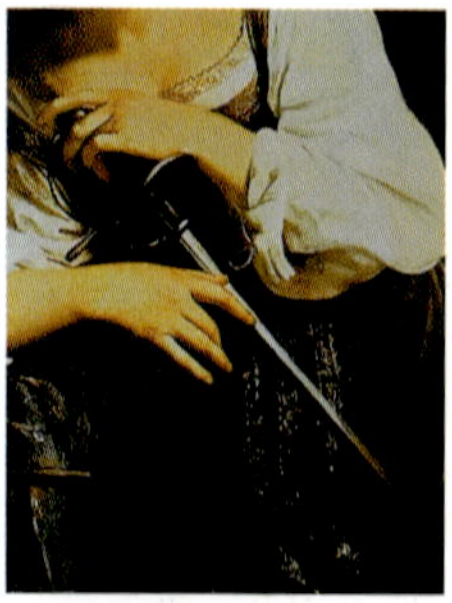

Caravaggio, *St Catherine*, Spain, Thyssen Bornmisza Museum, detail of rapier

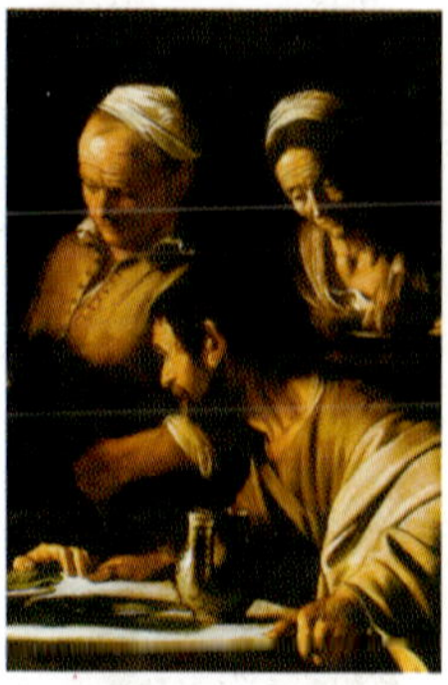

Caravaggio, *Supper at Emmaus*, Milan, Brera, detail

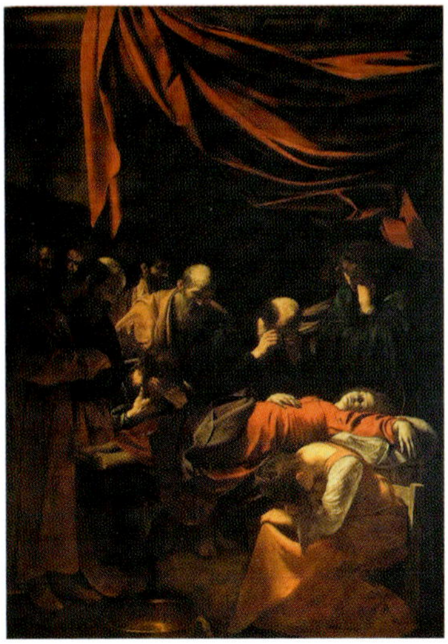

Caravaggio, *Death of the Virgin*, Paris, Louvre

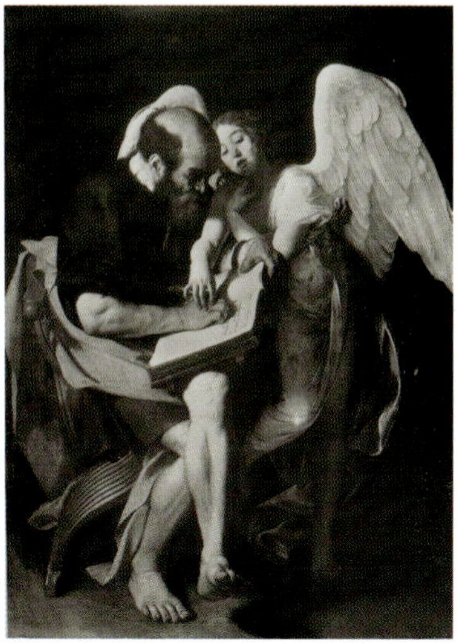

Caravaggio, *St Matthew*, formerly in Berlin, Kaiser Friedrich Museum

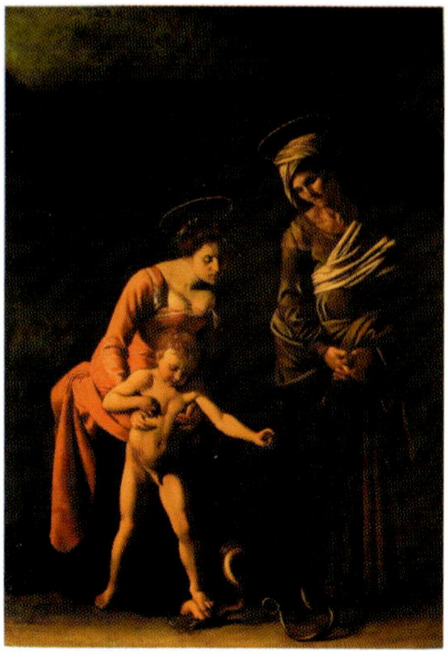

Caravaggio, *Madonna dei Palafrenieri*, Rome, Galleria Borghese

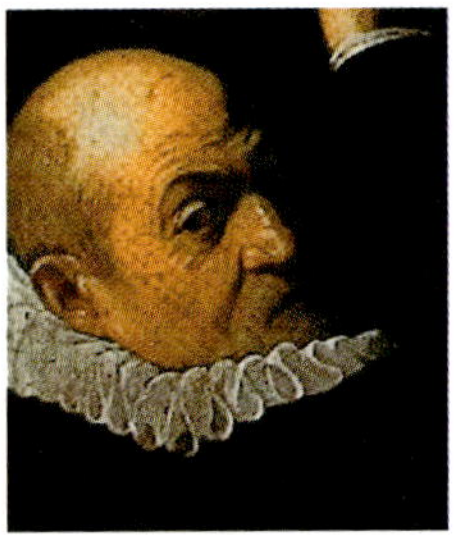

Caravaggio, *Our Lady of the Rosary*, Vienna, Kunsthistorisches Museum, presumed portrait of the Spanish Viceroy in Naples

but at one point Tommasoni fell to the ground. As he withdrew Caravaggio who had aimed at Tommasoni's thigh caught him in the stomach. Tommasoni died during the night from the wound that Caravaggio inflicted upon him but Caravaggio was also badly wounded. This was a serious crime – Caravaggio had to flee from Rome to escape from the jurisdiction of the Roman courts and the revenge of the Tomassoni family. He quickly moved out of the city heading south-west in search of protection. He was perhaps expecting to be pardoned by the Pope for his crimes which however failed to materialize. Caravaggio was then a penniless artist whose self-imposed exile must have been fraught with a sense of anguish and guilt. A *bando capitale* was issued against him – anybody could arrest him and bring him to justice in Rome. Captors often preferred to decapitate such bandits and present only the heads. These very circumstances led him to move south towards Naples where he arrived by October 1606.

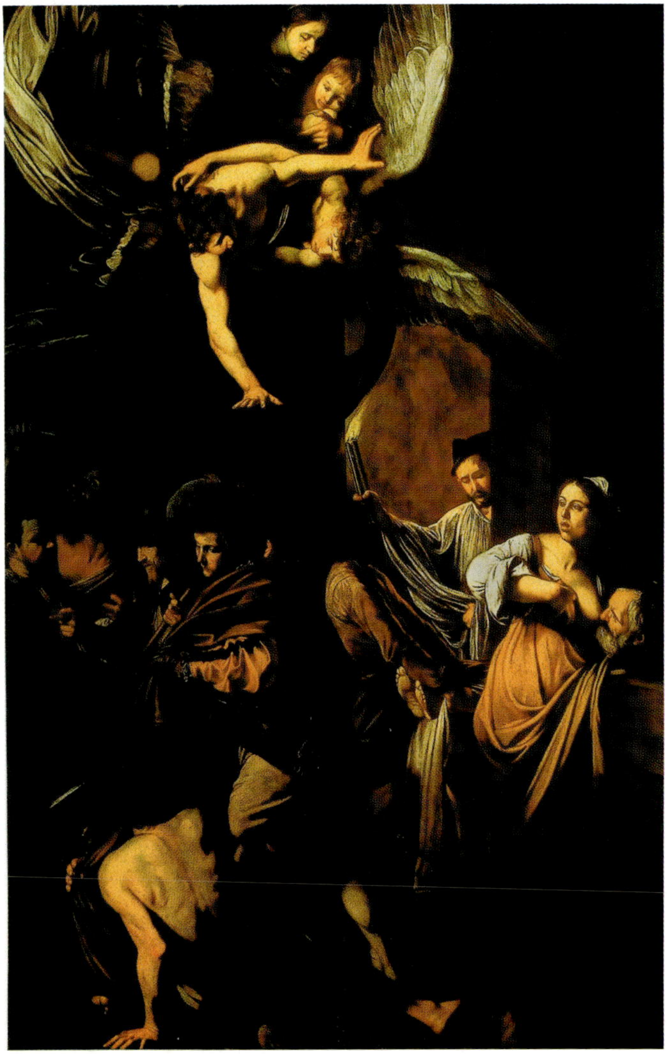

Caravaggio, *Seven Acts of Mercy*, Naples, Pio Monte della Misericordia

Naples was then part of the vast domains of the Spanish King Philip III. It was a commercial city three times the size of Rome but made safe by an imposing Spanish garrison. Caravaggio's fame had already spread South and the novelty of his art was known in the city. No Neapolitan artist could however match Caravaggio. His unique style immediately attracted the attention of the Duke of Benevente, the Spanish viceroy in the city who commissioned him for important works. Caravaggio was still a fugitive from Papal Rome but his art was placing him in good stead to win the favours of powerful politicians. Commissions began to pour in and his inventiveness and power of synthesis of complex subjects suggest that he set to work with enthusiasm and determination in spite of his self-brought on misfortunes.

By June 1607 Caravaggio seems to have made up his mind to leave Naples. He must have been attracted to Malta – becoming a knight could have meant that challenges such as the one presented to Giuseppe Cesari, the Cavalier d'Arpino, could not be unheeded again or ignored. The galleys of the Order of St John led by General Fabrizio Sforza Colonna were then in harbour for a brief stop on their way South to Malta. The island, then their headquarters or convent, was strategically sited on the periphery of Catholic Europe overlooking the

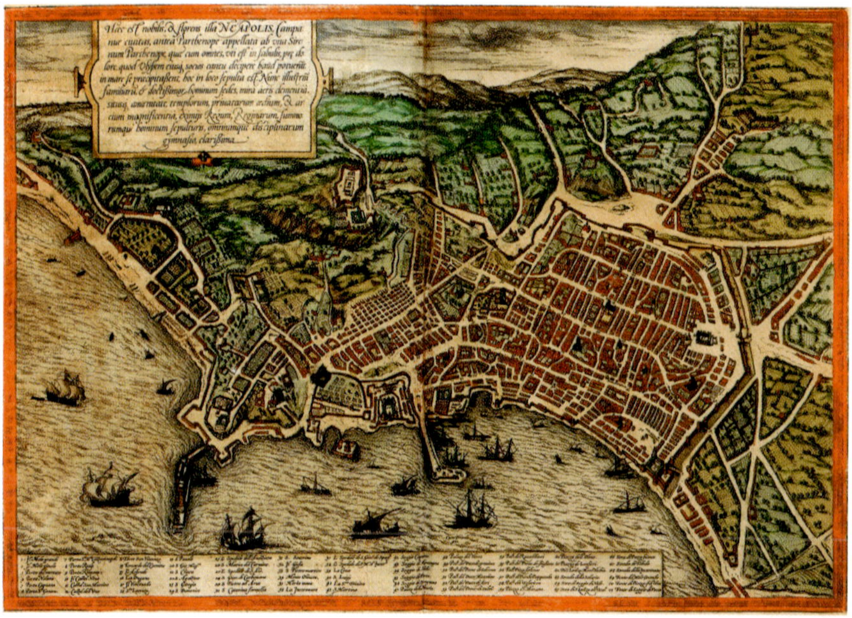

1572 map of Naples, (Braun and Hogenberg)

Ottoman territory. Granted to the Order of St John in fief by Charles V of Spain in 1530, Malta had sustained a heavy siege in 1565 from which it had emerged victorious. But the country was left in ruins yet inhabited by a community resolute enough to start building a long-planned new city that was to take the name of the hero of the siege – Grand Master Jean Parisot de La Vallette. Many knights remembered the onslaughts of those terrible days and had immortalised the happenings in the Grand Council chamber of the Magisterial Palace of Valletta. Sporadic attacks by corsairs on the island reminded them of their quest against the Ottomans and spurred them on to build more towers and military structures. The island was far from being at the centre of the artistic world yet Caravaggio might have also believed that powerful friends and connections could put him back in good stead to win papal pardon for the homicide he had committed in Rome.

The galleys left Naples shortly after the feast of St John the Baptist celebrated on 24th June. The journey to Malta was indeed adventurous; the then reigning Grand Master Fra Alof de Wignacourt had sent notice to his approaching galleys of enemy vessels lying in wait off the island of Gozo. All men were rallied and armed ready for a naval engagement that never materialised and the fleet sailed safely into harbour in July 1607. Caravaggio soon attracted the attention of the Grand Master and high ranking Knights of St John. He had travelled on the galleys with Fra Ippolito Malaspina who was soon to acquire from Caravaggio a painting representing St Jerome. Caravaggio's talents were immediately recognised and the Grand Master became resolute to bestow him with a knighthood. Yet Caravaggio's candidature was marred by circumstances. He was a fugitive fleeing from Rome after committing murder and was not of noble birth. Wignacourt had also pledged not to institute any more knights in the rank of magisterial obedience. The Grand Master was nonetheless resolute not to loose him and petitioned the Pope for a special one-off dispensation with which he could elect a painter who had committed murder as a knight of magisterial obedience.

Caravaggio, *Portrait of Aloph de Wignacourt*, Paris, Louvre, detail

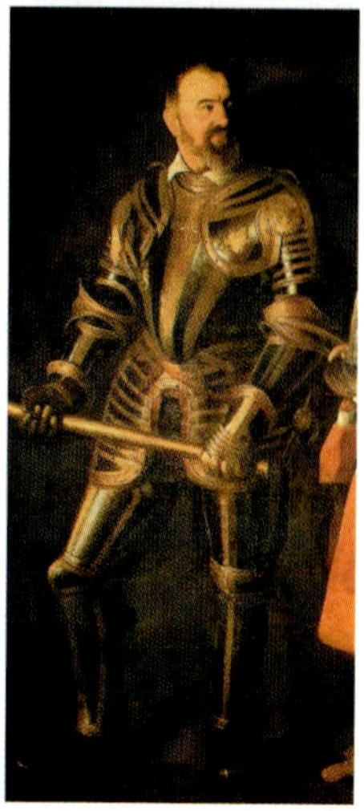

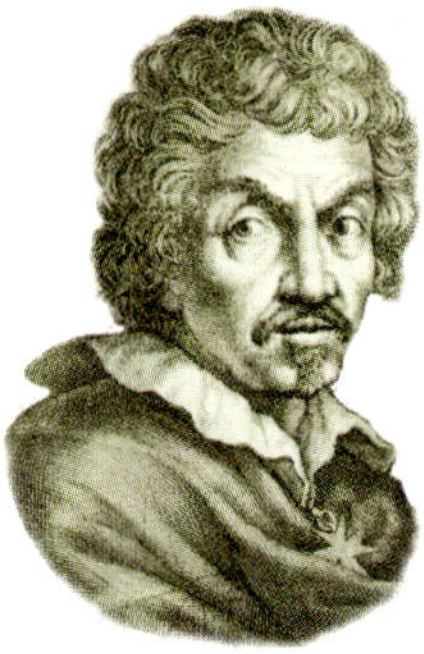

Bellori's *Portrait of Caravaggio*

Caravaggio became a knight of the Order of St John on 14th July 1608 in the Oratory of the Beheading in the former conventual church of St Johns that was shortly afterwards to house his only signed painting representing the martyrdom of St John the Baptist, the patron saint of the Order to which he now belonged. Grand Master Wignacourt awarded him with a much coveted golden chain and two slaves.

Yet again Caravaggio's furious character brought him trouble. Brawls were not uncommon in Malta; the home of arrogant young nobility prone to mischievous deeds and who were constantly fighting on land and at sea with the Ottomans. On 18th August 1608, a fight involving seven Italian knights including Caravaggio broke out in the residence of the Knight Prospero Coppini, the organist of the then conventual church of St John. The door of Coppini's house was broken down and a shot from a dangerous firearm mortally wounded Fra Giovanni Rodomonte Roero. An investigation ensued and Caravaggio was among the first to be arrested; two days before the feast of the Beheading of St John the Baptist. It was during this feast, celebrated on 29th August, that the large canvas of the Beheading of St John the Baptist was to be presented for public viewing. Caravaggio was kept in custody at Fort St Angelo – the fort from where the hero of the Great Siege Grand Master La Vallette had guided his troops to victory and that had since then lost much of its former glory. From St Angelo Caravaggio carried out a daring and successful escape scaling down its walls by means of ropes and immediately sought swift refuge to Sicily on a boat.

News of his escape was already known by 6th October. Powerful friends might have helped him to leave Malta but his deed was not acceptable. He had violated the statutes of the Order by leaving the island without the permission of the Grand Master. In December 1608 Caravaggio was expelled from the Order in front of his only signed painting completed a few weeks prior. By this time Caravaggio was in Syracuse. His hope of a papal pardon that failed to materialise and his mishaps with the order of St John left him with few possibilities – indeed all hope seemed lost and Caravaggio begun to seriously fear for his life. He oftentimes went to bed with his clothes and his dagger close at hand. He did however visit the heritage sites of the city including what was then the prison of Dyonisius but which Caravaggio re-named the Ear of Dyonisius. It is the name that still survives to-date that provided a functional explanation to a natural phenomenon.

But Caravaggio had to move shortly afterwards to the Sicilian city of Messina due to some mishaps that he was accused of. Messina was then the seat of administration of the Spanish Viceroy

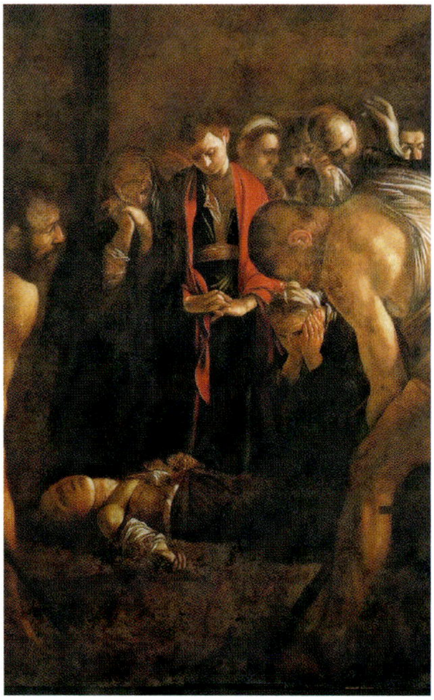

Caravaggio, *Burial of St Lucy*, Syracuse, Church of Santa Lucia al Sepolcro, detail

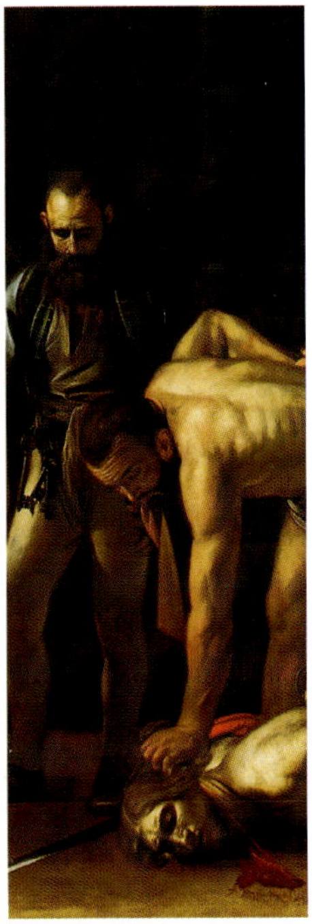

Caravaggio, *Beheading of St John the Baptist*, Valletta, St John's Co-Cathedral, detail

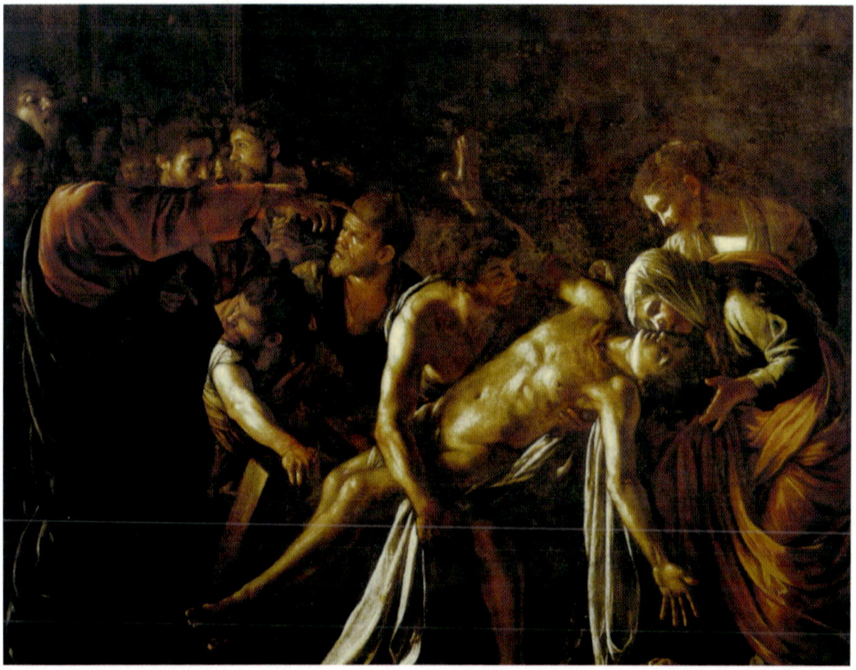

Caravaggio, *Raising of Lazarus*, Messina, Museo Regionale, detail

and one of the Order's most important priory then led by the newly appointed Knight Antonio Martelli. Caravaggio apparently roamed uninhibited around the city inspite of the presence of the Order of St John even though Grand Master Wignacourt could have spared no efforts in trying to capture him. He was still referred to as a knight of Malta and might have been protected yet again by powerful friends such as the Lazzari, a wealthy Genoese family based in Messina. Caravaggio might have found a new sense of hope for his misfortunes that could have led to his rebirth as a free man pardoned of his bad deeds. But Caravaggio was by now considered a demented artist; mad and fiendish, excessive in his every action. Following a brief stay in the Sicilian capital Palermo, the artist started on his last journey back to Naples where he spent a further eight months. He may have known that a papal pardon was a likely possibility but his fortunes yet again worsened. On his way to Naples he was surprised by a band of armed men who abused, battered and scarred him in the face. News of the deed reached Naples, many claimed that he had been disfigured or, worse still, killed. By the end of June 1610, he put his belongings on a felucca and set sail from Naples arriving close to the small town of Porto Ercole near Rome. The Spanish guards mistook the artist for somebody that they were lying in wait for to arrest and threw him into prison. Released a few days later he realised that the felucca had departed with his possessions on board leaving him behind. He started out on foot in the terrible heat of July 1610 in a state of utmost desperation and fury. He arrived in Porto Ercole but the scorching July sun proved to be fatal. He died a few days later struck by a malignant fever. The much-coveted papal pardon was announced a few days later.

An epitaph written by Marzio Milesi; a jurist and friend of Caravaggio reads

Michaelangelo Merisi da Caravaggio
– Jerosolomitan knight –
eminent emulator of nature …
died 18 July 1610.

Caravaggio, *David and Goliath*, Rome, Galleria Borghese, detail of Goliath as self-portrait

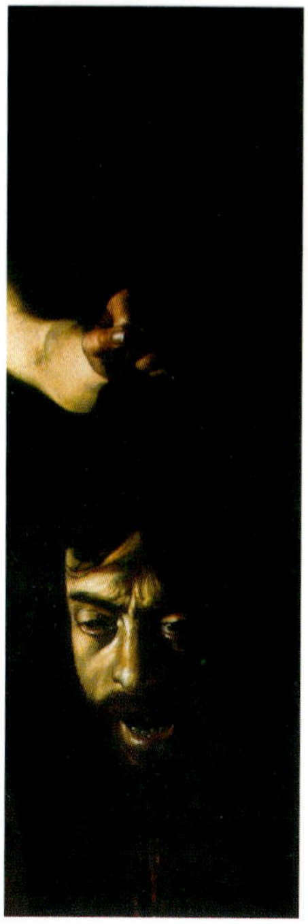

Caravaggio's Malta

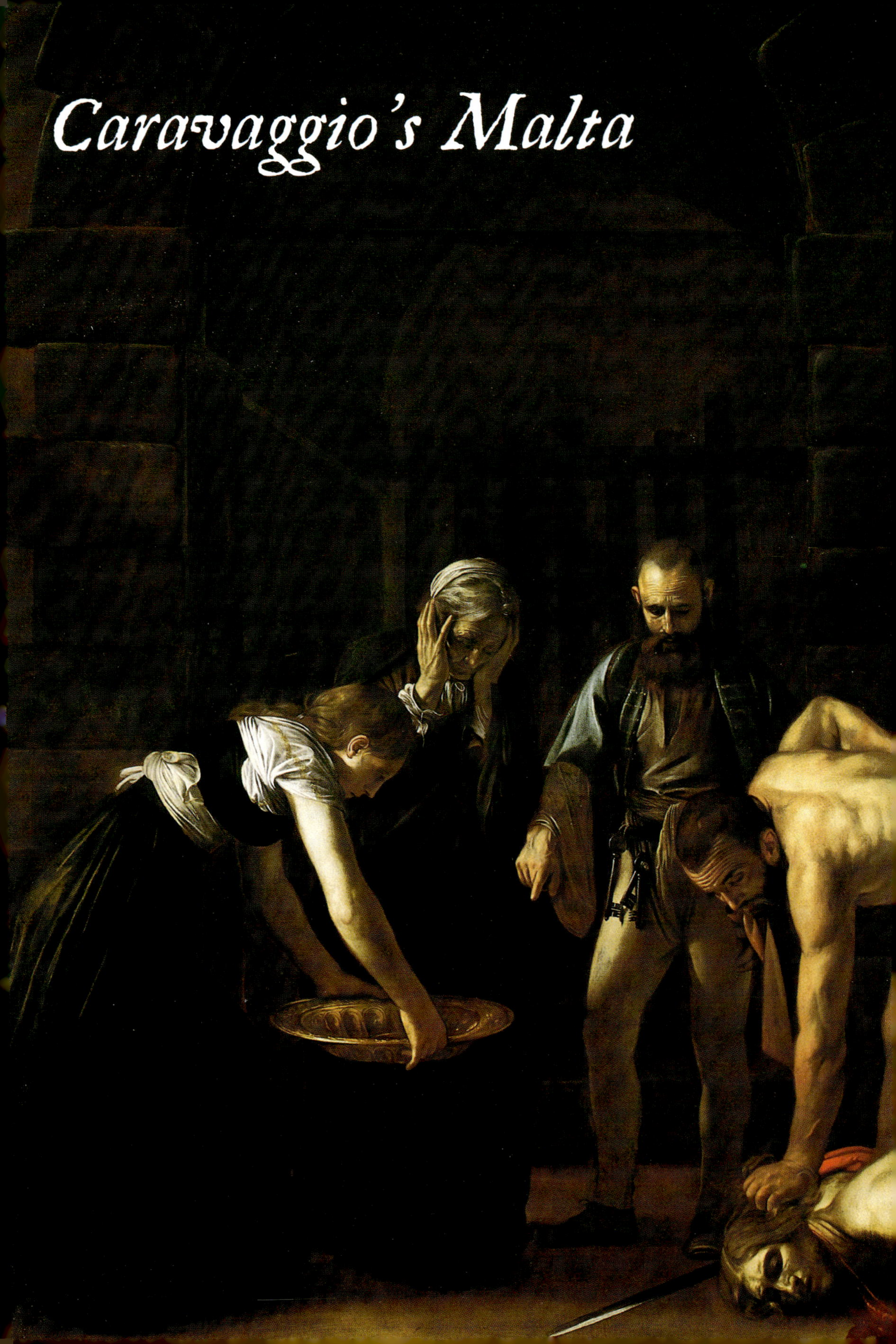

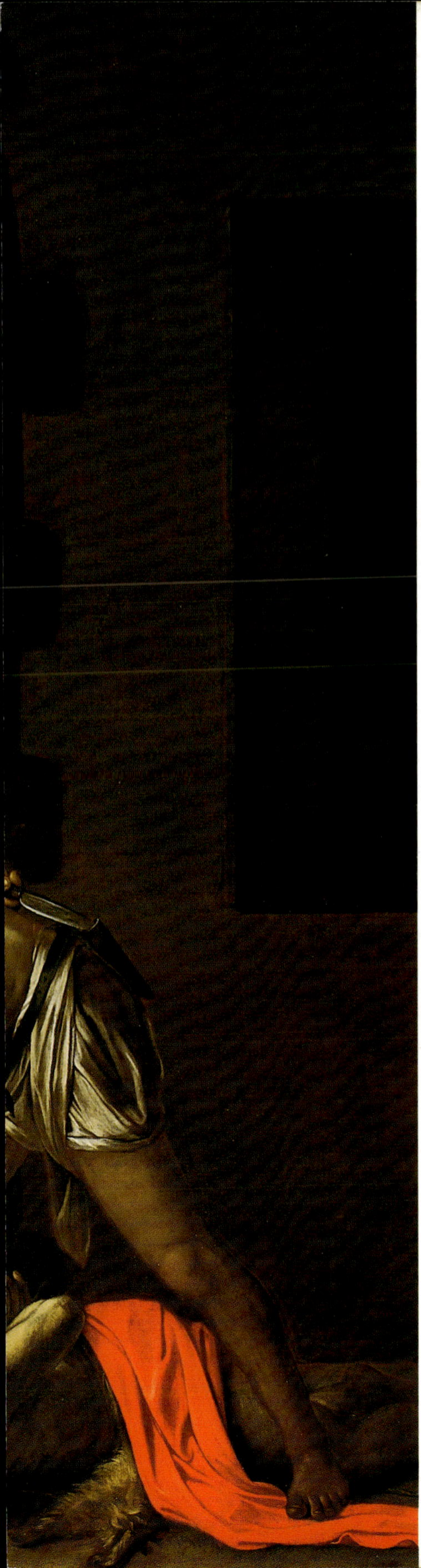

Caravaggio's arrival in Malta 400 years ago on 12th July 1607 was not a celebrated event as the paintings left behind now are. He had left Naples with the fleet of the knights of the Order of St John under the command of Knight Fabrizio Sforza Colonna, captain general of the galleys and a personal acquaintance of Caravaggio. Together with the fleet a newly built galley was on its maiden voyage from Marseille to Malta.[1] Naples was indeed one of the ports of call for the Order's fleet in the western Mediterranean and happenings in Naples were likely to be known in Malta through visitors travelling to and from Naples and Malta through Sicily. The sons of the Spanish Viceroy, the Duke of Benevente, are known to have travelled to Malta before and also after Caravaggio's arrival in Malta.[2] Caravaggio's plight and arrival could have been already known also through knights travelling to and from Naples.

Grand Harbour was considered one of the finest safe havens in the Mediterranean, much more so with the building of the new fortified city of Valletta completed a few years earlier in response to the plight of the Great Siege of 1565. The population was mainly concentrated in the harbour area; an extended city, sited on three peninsulas including Valletta, Vittoriosa and Senglea. The inhabitants were a mixture of locals and foreigners including a relatively small population of knights and members of the Order of St John living in Malta.[3] The locals included the Maltese merchant class, the rich and the intelligencia of the island, easily distinguishable from other locals through their dress.[4] It is to this urban area that the inhabitants from the countryside were attracted mainly because of a better opportunity to earn a living and

Caravaggio, *Beheading of St John the Baptist*, Valletta, St John's Co-Cathedral, detail

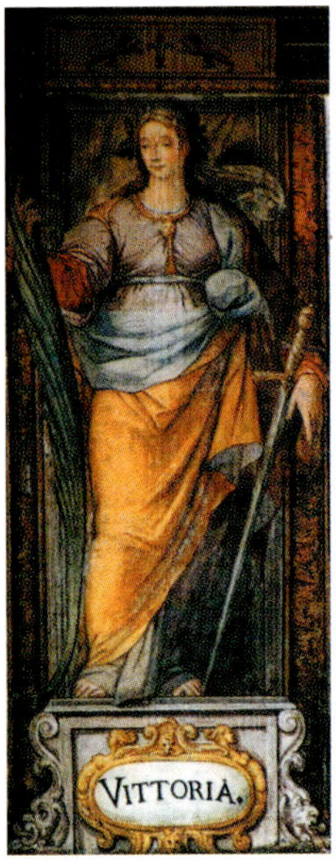

Matteo Perez d'Aleccio, *Great Siege Cycle of Mural Paintings*, Valletta, Grand Master's Palace, Allegorical figure of Victory, detail

the security of better defences in case of a sudden attack on the islands by the Ottomans. The Great Siege of 1565 was indeed still vivid in the memories of many. Furthermore, the event had been immortalised in a cycle of frescoes painted by Matteo Perez d'Aleccio for the Grand Council Chamber. The cycle, almost reminiscent of a script or an eulogising sermon such as the one celebrated each year on the eve of 8th September,[5] had been produced to great detail not only with regards to the happenings of the siege but also to the Ottoman forces, the marching formation of particular regiments and the representation of both Janissaries and regular Turkish infantry. Memories of the siege were still in the minds of many and not to be forgotten.

At the beginning of the seventeenth century, the island was ruled by a tripartite power structure including Bishop, Grand Master and Inquisitor. All sought Rome as the seat of their authority although the island remained a fiefdom of the Spanish crown ever since having been granted to the Order by Charles V of Spain in 1530. The island had undergone a relative process of political de-sicilianisation through efforts were mainly promoted by Grand Masters Jean de la Cassiere (1572-81) and Hugh Loubens de Verdalle (1581-95) but commercial and kinship links with Sicily remained largely intact. Sicilian wine was still Malta's own wine to such an extent as to account for the lack of a local viticulture industry.[6] Visitors to the island also identified Malta as an extension of mainland Italy rather than African.[7]

Grand Master Alof de Wignacourt was a veteran of the battle of Lepanto (1571) who had previously held important posts within the Langue of France mainly related to the management of the Order's Sacra Infermeria. His entourage and close circle of friends included knights who were to patronise Caravaggio.[8] Knight Francesco dell'Antella, Wignacourt's

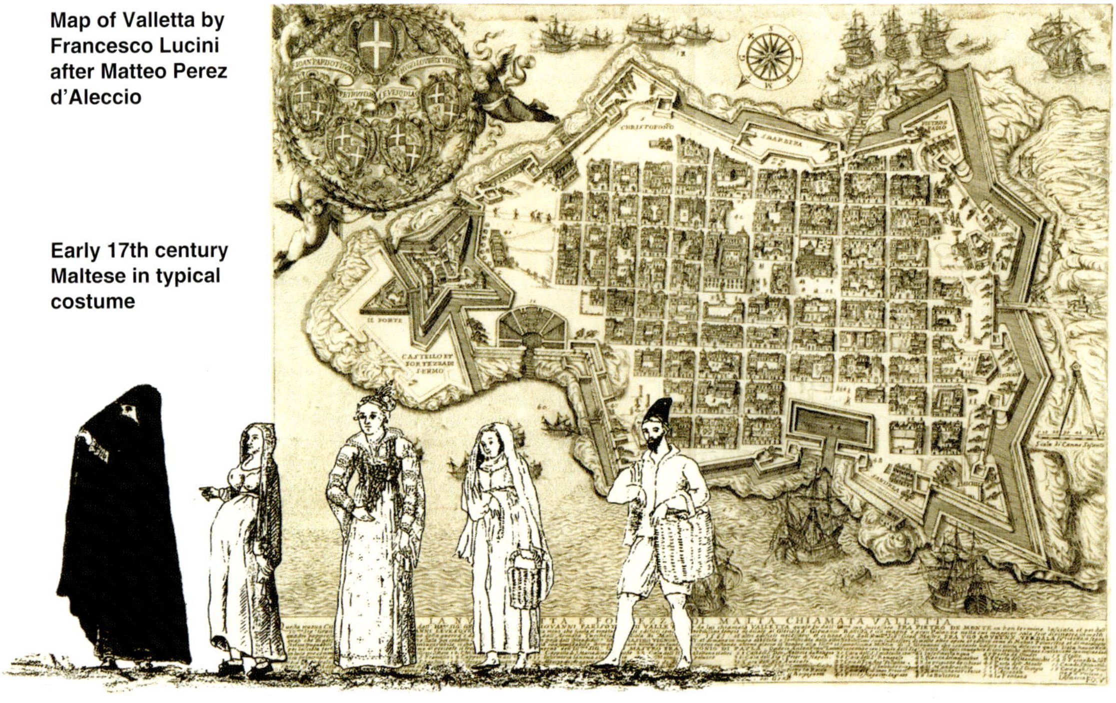

Map of Valletta by Francesco Lucini after Matteo Perez d'Aleccio

Early 17th century Maltese in typical costume

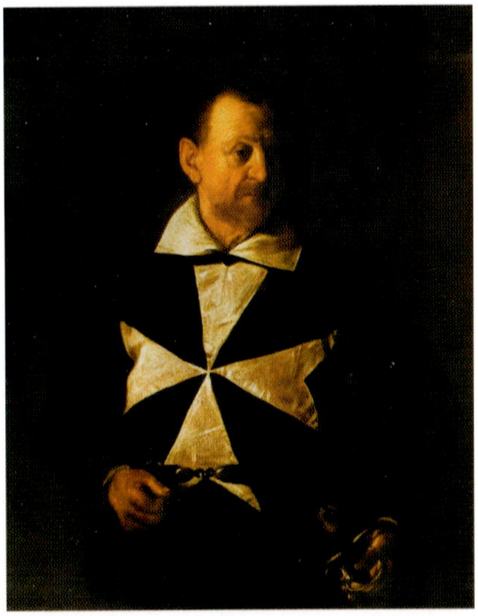

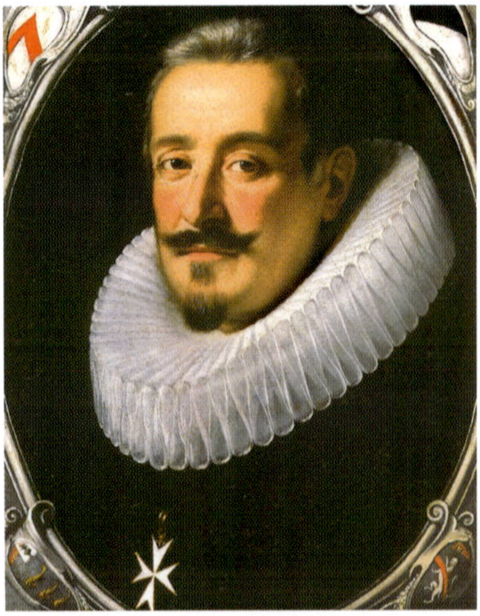

Left: Caravaggio, presumed *Portrait of the Knight Antonio Martelli*, Florence, Pitti

Right: *Portrait of the Knight Francesco dell'Antella* by Justus Sustermans

young, influential Florentine secretary and a cultured man of letters, was to be the proud owner of Caravaggio's *Sleeping Cupid*. Wignacourt's great elector Knight Ippolito Malaspina, then the oldest member of the Order and intimate adviser to the Grand Master, was to own Caravaggio's *St Jerome* marked with Malaspina's coat-of-arms like other paintings presumably originating from his private collection. Malaspina had travelled to Malta on the same voyage as Caravaggio and was one of Wignacourt's close friends. The Knight Ottavio Martelli, another senior member of the Italian Langue, was a member of an illustrious Florentine family whose presumed portrait was probably painted by Caravaggio during his stay in Malta. Other works suggested or actually produced by Caravaggio on the island also relate directly to the Order's presence but Malta was not a completely sterile artistic world prior to Caravaggio's arrival. Filippo Paladini (1544-1616) and Matteo Perez d'Aleccio (1547-1616) had been commissioned by the Order to decorate its major palaces and churches. Shortly after Caravaggio's departure from Malta in 1609, the Order acquired the services of Lionello Spada (1576-1622) who was to paint episodes from the history of the Order for the Grand Master's palace. Visitors to the island comment on the fine interiors of the palaces then built in Valletta including elegant rooms decorated with exquisite hangings. Wignacourt himself is also known to have treated his guests to music during banquets revising a long- forgotten tradition last embraced by Grand Master Verdalle.

Out in the countryside, the population lived in extreme poverty. Social conditions were indeed low and many lived in low-roofed houses of limestone with flat roofs and few windows. Troglodythic settlements were still thriving. Fiduciary coins were still being minted and the circulation of low denomination coinage confirms that poverty was the norm not the exception.[9] The best wages were perhaps earned by those employed in the services of the Order.[10] Boatswains and shipmates on the Order's galley squadrons were paid 3 scudi a month in 1616. Those handling slaves on the Order's galleys would receive 22 tari a month in 1614. Four tari a day was the average wage of a masonry worker and hardly 10 families earned 600 scudi per annum. 50 families earned 200 scudi and the rest lived in poverty.[11] Demographic

Caravaggio, *St Jerome*, Valletta, St John's Co-Cathedral, detail of the coat-of-arms of Ippolito Malaspina

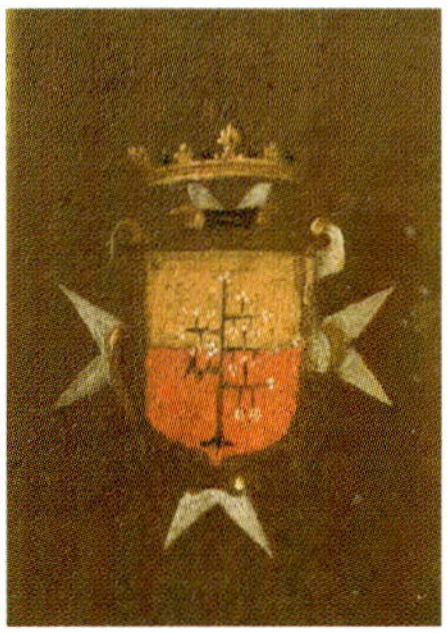

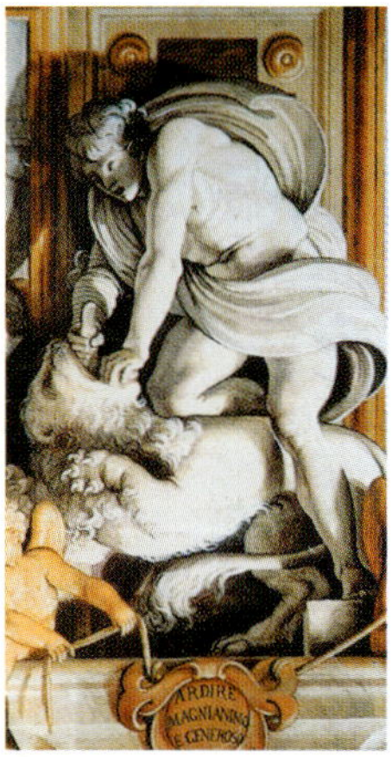

Lionello Spada, *History of the Order Cycle of Mural Paintings*, Valletta, Grand Master's Palace, Allegorical figure of Fortitude, detail

figures nonetheless suggest a relative general recovery. In 1614, eight years after Caravaggio's departure, the population numbered 41,000 in both Malta and Gozo, one fourth of which was concentrated in the harbour area. This means a sharp increase from the 25,000 mark registered for 1574 and which indeed suggests a demographic recovery. The population of the island of Gozo too was also slowly recovering from a depression brought about by a series of sustained attacks by the Ottomans on the island following the 1551 attack when practically all the island's population was taken into slavery. By the early 17th century, the population amounted to over 2,000 with the majority living in the citadel and its suburb.

In Malta, Italian was the language spoken most in the harbour area while the rest spoke Maltese as their native language. Parishes remained the fulcrum of everyday life in the villages and the parish priests also served as public officials registering births, deaths and marriages. Education was limited to a few and the clergy were generally the most literate knowing also how to write. There was a lack of books and the Inquisition ensured that prohibited books were retrieved from circulation. In May 1609, shortly after Caravaggio's escape from Malta by October 1608, a number of books deemed prohibited due to their contents were burned publicly in the main square of Vittoriosa.[12]

The laxity of the city dwellers was a major headache for the Inquisitor residing in Vittoriosa. Prostitution was rife albeit illegal and illegitimacy was high in the harbour area. Since the turn of the century, the inquisition had been focusing more on social and moral issues rather than schismatic concerns triggered by the divide between Protestants and Catholics. Caravaggio was called to witness by the Inquisitor Leonetto della Corbara on a case of suspected bigamy involving a Greek painter whose identity remains unknown.[13] Caravaggio's deposition is anything but informative since he had then pleaded ignorance of the case but it has been nonetheless of utmost importance in pinning down his Maltese period more precisely. From amongst those called to witness on the same case, knight Giacomo Marchese merits a particular mention. Of Sicilian extraction, Marchese had sailed to Malta from Messina on the same voyage as Caravaggio. Later in 1615, he was chosen by Wignacourt to raise troops in Sicily for the defence of Malta following news that the Ottomans were preparing another large-scale attack. Marchese might not have been so much of a backbencher as this particular task delegated by Wignacourt suggests that he was influential in Sicily. He owned a palace in Messina sited close to the harbour area. In 1628, Knight

Opposite: Detail from Lucini's representations of the Great Siege of Malta after Matteo d'Aleccio's frescoes

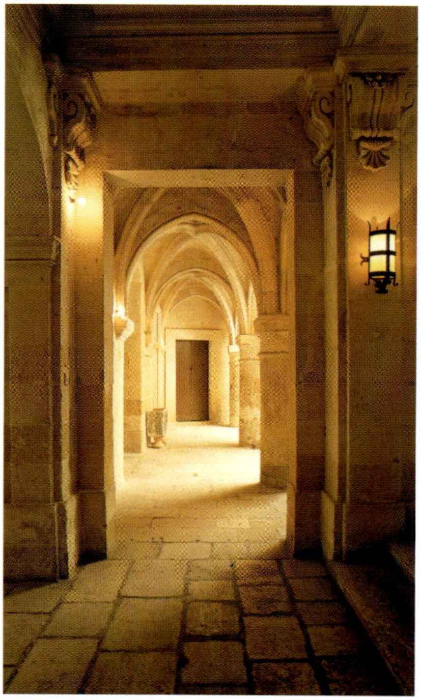

Inquisitor's Palace, Vittoriosa

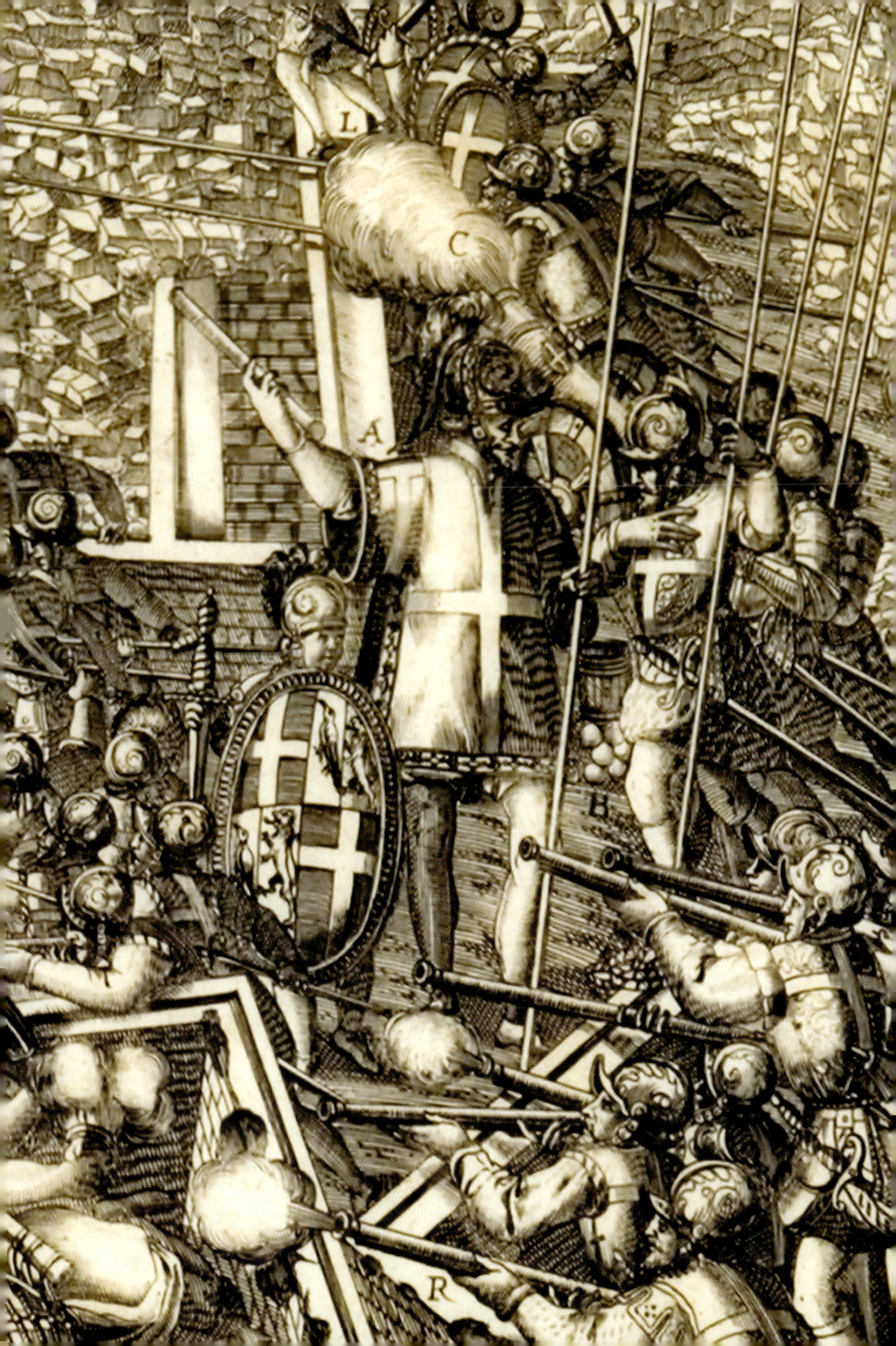
L
C
A
B
R

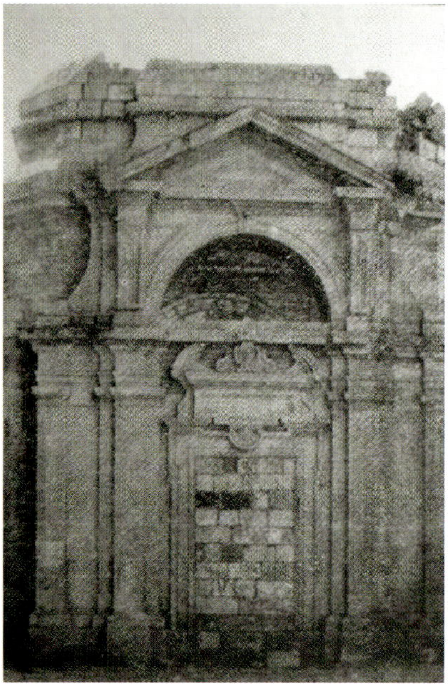

20th century photograph of the Nibbia Chapel, now destroyed

Giacomo Marchese is decribed as a Commendatore interested in setting up a new commandery within the Order (Commenda Marchese). In return he expected the Order to elevate him to Grand Cross (Gran Croce).[14]

The first decade of the 17th century witnessed the continuing construction of new buildings in Valletta. The monastic orders had by then built their convents and adjoining churches. The Carmelites, the Dominicans and the Franciscan Minors had completed their Valletta convents by the mid-1570s.[15] Through their contacts in Rome, the Dominicans had succeeded in raising their church to a parish through Pope Pius V in July 1571. Friction between the canons of Mdina cathedral and the Dominicans ensued and a second parish dedicated to St Paul's Shipwreck was set up in Valletta. The limits of these two parishes were still an open affair by the time Caravaggio arrived in Malta and the Dominicans were strongly asserting their claims. The foundation of the first Capuchin convent in Malta dates to 1588, mainly patronised by Grand Master Verdalle.[16] The last to build their convent in Valletta were the Franciscan Conventuals; seven years before Caravaggio's arrival in Malta in 1607 and the Discalced Carmelites were to arrive much later in 1625.[17]

In 1612, four years after Caravaggio's departure from Malta, the Chancellor of the Order, the Knight Pietro Gonzales de Mendoza, built a church in honour of the Apostle Saint James the Less also enriched by an altar painting representing the apostle saint painted by Filippo Paladini.[18] Other chapels were built by particular members of the Order of St John. In 1612, Knight Giorgio Nibbia was granted permission to build a chapel dedicated to Our Lady of Mercy near the Order's Hospital.[19] The Oratory of the Decollatio dedicated to the martyrdom of St John the Baptist was also built during the first quarter of the 17th century. It was purposely built for the members of the Confraternity of the Virgin of the Rosary of whom the majority were mainly members

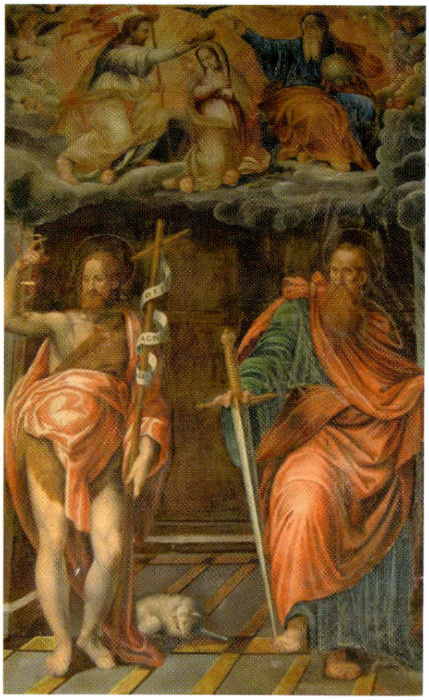

Late 16th century unknown artist, *Coronation of the Virgin with Sts. John the Baptist and Paul*, Vittoriosa, Inquisitor's Palace

Pope Pius V

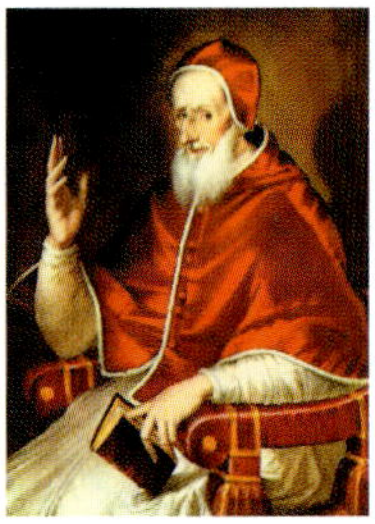

of the Order. Their confraternity was then based in the Oratory of the same dedication in the parish church of Our Lady of Safe Haven administered by the Dominicans. The Order had apparently urged them to re-organise themselves into a new Confraternity to be known as *Della Misericordia* [of mercy] and a commission was set up to gather the necessary funding and steer the project. The building was completed in December 1603 on a site offered to the brethren by Wignacourt himself. Its inauguration was marked by a solemn procession led by the then prior of the Conventual church of St John Pietro Urrea Camarasa, from the Oratory of the Rosary to the new Oratory accompanying the relic of the nasal bone of St John the Baptist. The old oratory dedicated to the Virgin of the Rosary had just been purchased by the Dominican fathers for 1360 scudi, a hefty sum of money which could not be paid outright and without difficulties.

By the time Caravaggio had probably started working on his large canvas of the Beheading of St John the Baptist, the Dominican fathers were being sued by the Confraternity of Mercy with the intention of retrieving their much needed money. Following a Papal Bull dated April 1608, the Confraternity of Mercy sued the Dominicans through the then Inquisitor Leonetto della Corbara and the outcome dated 20th August 1608 was decided against the Dominicans. The final installment of 100 scudi was however only paid by the Dominican fathers in July 1614.

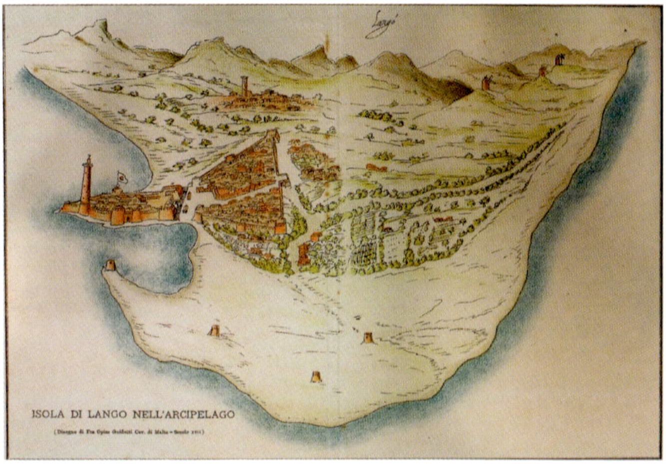

Map of 17th century Lango

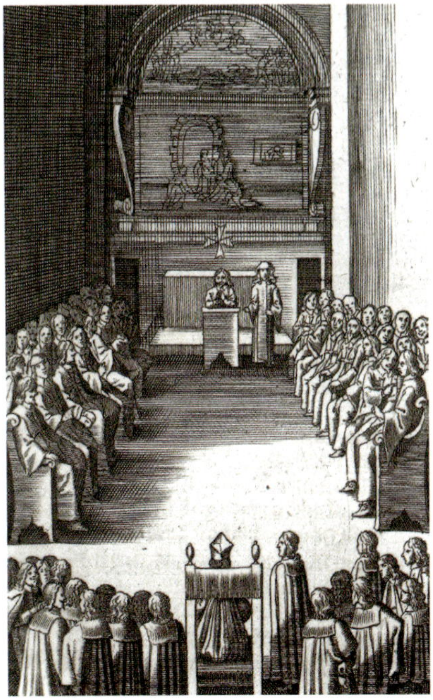

17th century image of the Oratory of St John from an engraving by C. von Osterhausen, Augsburg, 1650

The Ottoman threat

Three sequential quests against the Ottomans shortly after Wignacourt's accession to the Magistracy suggest a concerted effort that was to renovate the crusading spirit of the Order. In 1602, the Order attacked the town of Mahomett (Hammamet, Tunisia). The fleet and its ground troops carried out a lightening attack capturing the town and taking its inhabitants into slavery. A year later, the Order's fleet attacked Patras (Patras, Greece) and Lepanto (Nafpaktos, Greece) which they won with surprisingly few casualties. In 1604, the Order's fleet attacked the island of Lango in the Aegean Sea which was a

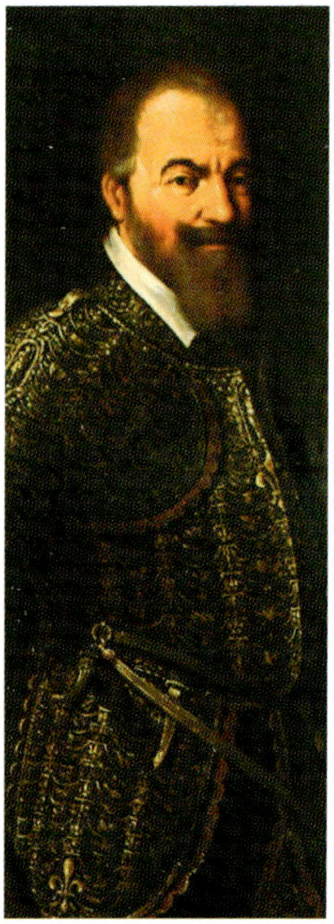

Anonymous author, *Portrait of Grand Master Alof de Wignacourt*, Valletta, National Museum of Fine Arts, detail

former possession of the Order. These were not isolated circumstances at the beginning of Wignacourt's magistracy. The attack on Laiazzo (Yumurtalik, Turkey) in 1610 was perhaps the most daring carried out during his magistracy. A selection of these quests was later commemorated with inscriptions on the Neptune's Fountain constructed near Porta del Monte close to the church of Our Lady of Liesse. The fountain was also sited opposite the galley harbour between Vittoriosa and Senglea and related well with its then surrounding landscape.[20]

The gates of the captured cities were presented to the icon of Our Lady of Philermos at the former conventual church of St John's where silver plaques still commemorate these military achievements. But the quest against the Ottomans continued and during Caravaggio's stay in Malta, Sforza Colonna did not fail to distinguish himself. Sources record the entry of a vessel captured by Sforza Colonna in April 1608 together with 77 slaves. He was later to enter harbour in May 1608 with further booty then including 21 slaves, oil, bails of linen and other materials. A few weeks later in July, Fra Guidotti returned to Malta with captured Ottoman vessels loaded with 74 slaves and cereals. Shortly before Caravaggio's arrival in Malta, Fra Guidotti had also captured a large number of slaves in Cypriot waters and a hefty sum of money. The booty then included a quantity of pearls; two noteworthy ones were kept aside with the most prized possessions of the Order. Other quests against the Ottomans were also carried out at the expense of Grand Master Wignacourt who in 1602 personally fitted a galleon against the Ottomans.

Naval encounters were not always successful and the new galley built in Marseille then accompanied to Malta by the Order's fleet was seen

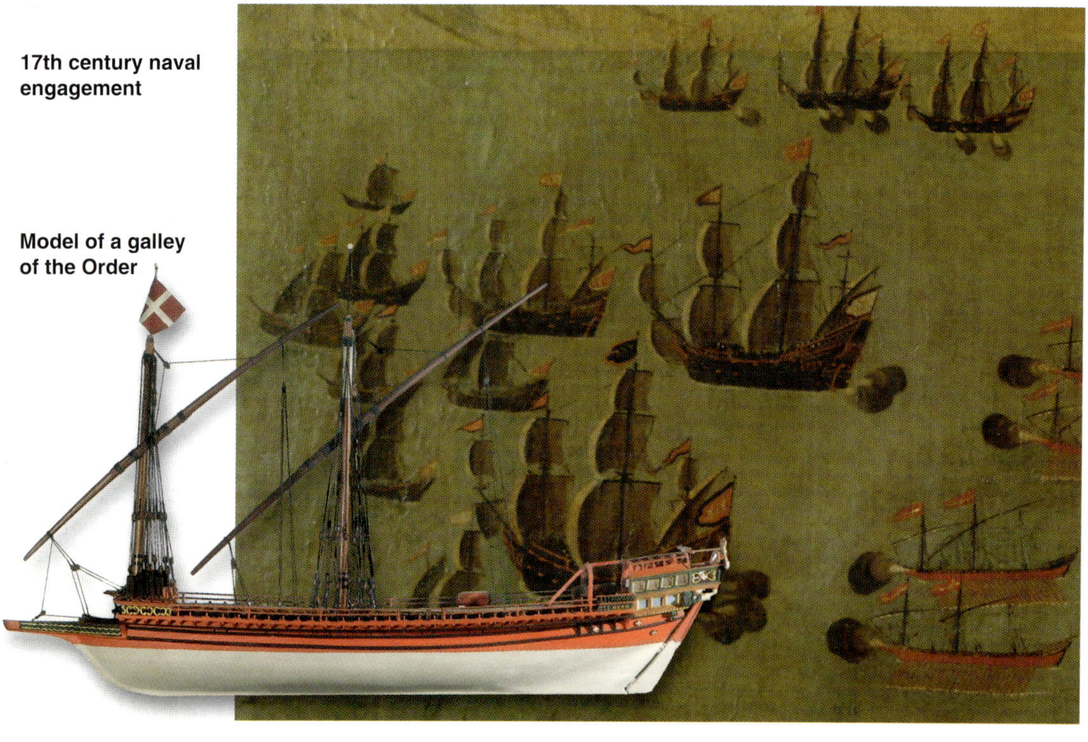

17th century naval engagement

Model of a galley of the Order

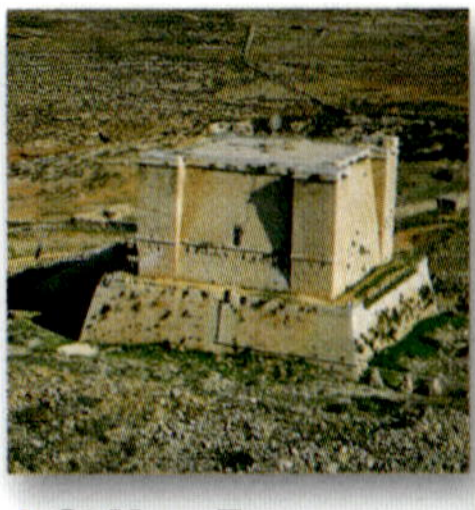

1. **St Mary Tower**
Comino

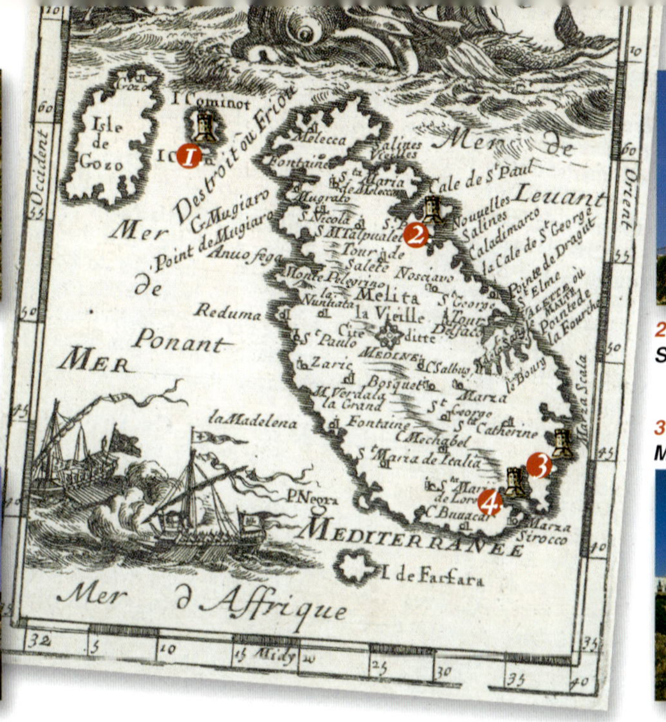

2. **Wignacourt Tower**
St Paul's Bay

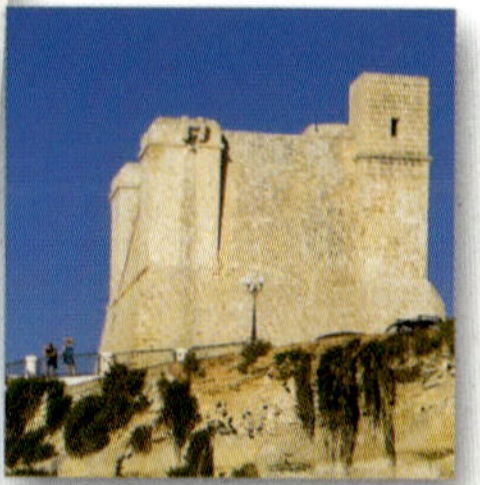

4. **St Lucian Tower**
Marsaxlokk

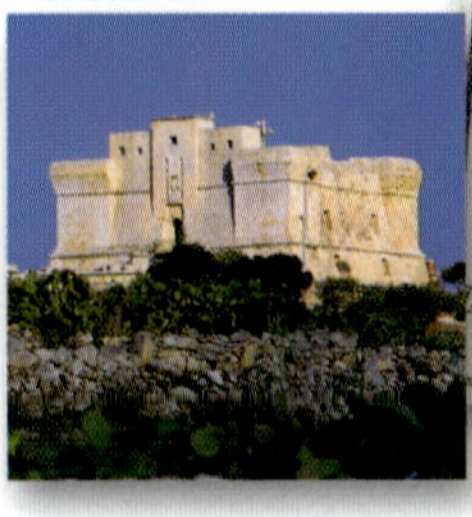

3. **St Thomas Tower**
Marsaskala

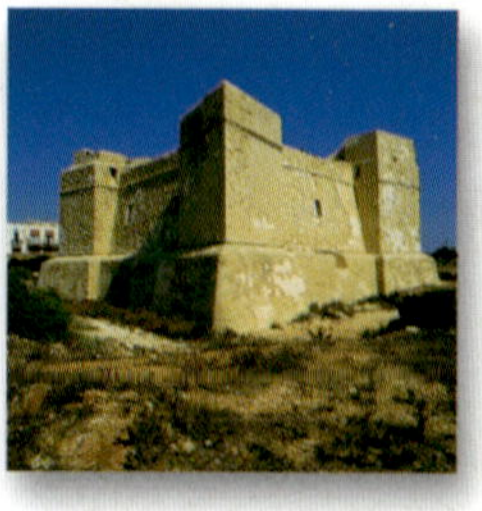

Map showing fortifications by Grand Master Wignacourt

as a welcome addition to the Order's depleted naval squadron. More than a year before Caravaggio's arrival in Malta in April 1606, the five galleys of the Order were caught in a storm while lying in wait for Ottoman vessels in a small bay of the island of Cimbalo (Zembra) in the Gulf of Tunis off Cape Bon. Three of the galleys, the *Capitana*, the *San Michele* and the *San Giorgio* were wrecked but their crews managed to swim ashore. Over the next fortnight, the shipwrecked crews suffered continuous attacks by the Ottomans; forty men were killed or taken prisoners and all the slaves escaped before any rescue expedition could be sent.[21] Such a loss was indeed unexpected but the Order was not left alone. The King of Spain donated a new galley built at Naples and an old disarmed one from Palermo. Donations were forwarded by the Captain-General himself who gave 6,000 scudi to help defray the expenses for constructing a new *Capitana*. Wignacourt also donated 10,000 scudi towards this much needed re-construction.

It is only after Caravaggio's departure from Malta that Wignacourt's extensive militarisation projects for the defence of the island gained full swing. The project for the building of a tower in St Paul's Bay was presented in Council in November 1609. The fort was to be built at the expense of Wignacourt at a cost of 6,748 scudi. A second tower was proposed by Wignacourt for Marsaxlokk bay (St Lucian's Tower) in July 1610. The hefty cost totalling 11,745 scudi was yet again made good by Wignacourt in his personal capacity and the tower was completed a few months later. The cost of their construction was immense and they probably related to news of fresh attacks by the Ottomans on Malta. The roll calls of the militia during the second decade of the 17th century also confirm this concern.[22] The 1614 attack of the Ottomans on the island was pushed back and the enemy could only pillage the countryside around Zejtun. It was nonetheless the reason behind the building of a fort in Marsascala (St Thomas' Tower)

Willem Shellinks, Neptune's Fountain, Valletta

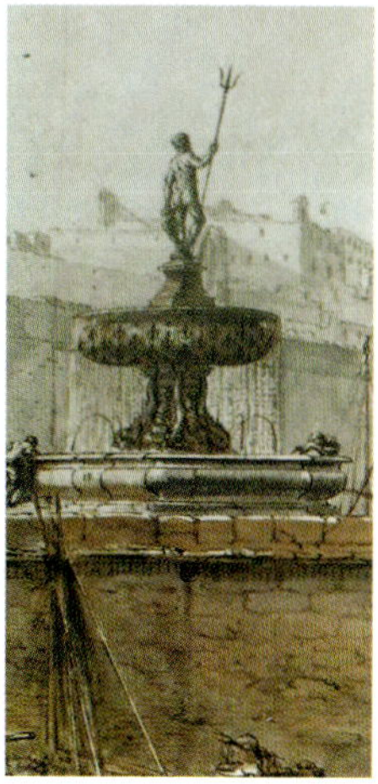

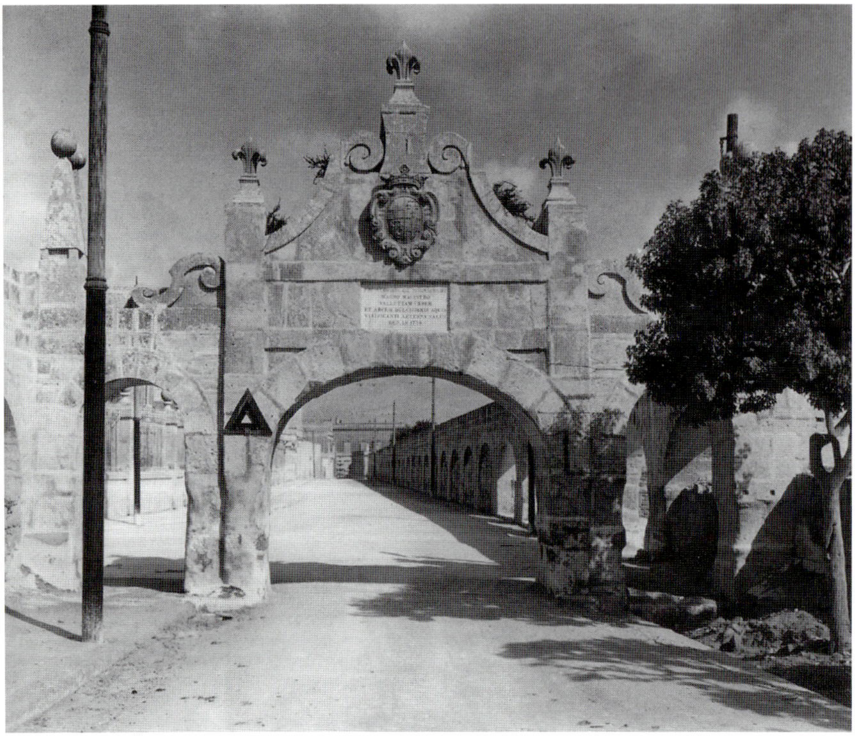

Former archway of Wignacourt's aqueduct

shortly afterwards and a further Fort in Comino (St Mary's Tower) built by Wignacourt in October 1618. The event was later commemorated in a painting in the style of Caravaggio representing the *Martyrdom of St Catherine of Alexandria* to serve as the titular piece for the old parish church of Zejtun. A further fort named after the Virgin of Graces was also built near Zabbar by Wignacourt.

Part of the surviving tract of Wignacourt's aqueduct

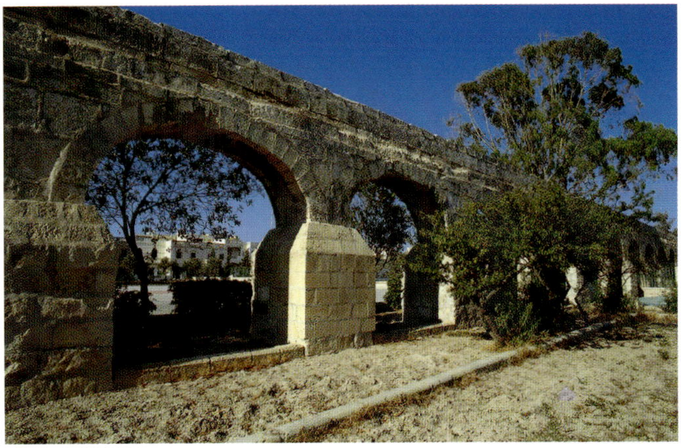

The aqueduct built to carry water from the countryside around Mdina to Valletta in itself also falls in line with these general plans for the defence of the island.[23] Sources confirm that water shortages in Valletta were constant and plans to build an aqueduct had been proposed earlier in 1596 during the Magistracy of Fra Martino Garzes. Seasons of draught often meant dry wells that could create serious problems for the inhabitants of the city even though water cisterns were obligatory for every household. When dry winters caused this deficiency, water would be carried on special barges from Marsa. A decision to build an aqueduct was deliberated in January 1610, a few months after Wignacourt had proposed to build the towers of St Paul's Bay and Marsascala. The project was also patronised by Wignacourt in his private capacity and took 600 workers to complete by 1615. Water sprouting for the first time in the fountain appositely built in front of the palace was welcomed with great rejoicing by the population of the city.

Personal Vicissitudes

The military quests of the Order's members must have probably augmented rather than eased their military character which oftentimes turned into aggressive behaviour when back in convent. Wignacourt was more often than not concerned with the frequent fights in which the knights did get involved but could probably do little more than nothing to contain the situation. The transfer of the armoury to the palace by Wignacourt in 1604 could also be in line with these efforts although the main reason was probably lack of space. The armoury grew and by 1617 contained enough arms to equip 12,000 soldiers. Efficiency in its maintenance and upkeep also meant that 2,000 men could be made ready at any hour. But armaments then in circulation were expected to be collected and access restricted and the transfer to the palace also meant the availability of larger spaces where the armoury could grow and expand.[24] Prohibitions against carrying lethal weapons were also endorsed. As early as 1568, any knight caught in possession of a weapon other than his sword and dagger was bound to loose two years of seniority. A specific order against carrying wheel-lock pistols was issued in 1597.

A public brawl in which Caravaggio became involved was thus not an isolated case and regulations were still going unheeded. Caravaggio's character and his wrongdoings were not unknown and had been one of two reasons for which Wignacourt had requested a dispensation from the Pope to be able to knight him. Some of the other members of the Order involved in the brawl were also not free from misdeeds.[25] Fra Prospero Coppini, a member of the German Langue, whose front door was smashed during the tumultuous events, had earlier in 1590 committed a joint murder with another knight. This time he was relatively innocent of mischief. Another perpetrator, the knight Giulio Accarigi – the future admiral and head of the Italian Langue, had previously committed two murders and was apparently a known trouble maker. But it is Pietro di Ponte who was armed and eventually injured the victim, the Knight Rodomonte Roero. Such misdeeds rarely went unpunished and the defrocking (*privatio habitum*) of knights were not one off circumstances even though such decisions could indeed be reversed. Fra Prospero Coppini was defrocked for a crime he committed in 1590 but was re-admitted into the Order in 1592. Since 1568, anybody handling firearms after dusk was also liable to a *privatio habitum*. Pietro di Ponte was defrocked but readmitted into the Order after a few years. The fate of the three knights responsible for the murder of

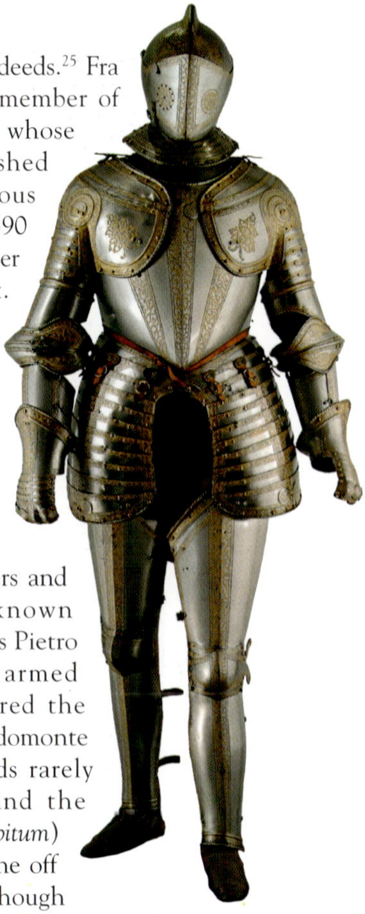

Jean Jacques de Verdelin's suit-of-armour featuring in Caravaggio's portrait of Wignacourt

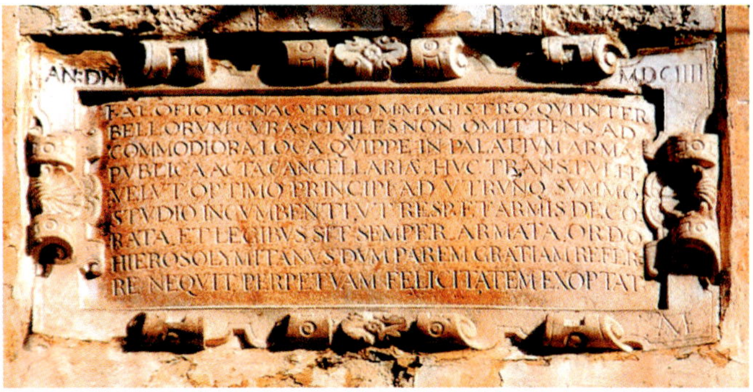

Inscription in stone commemorating the transfer of the Armoury to the Palace in 1604

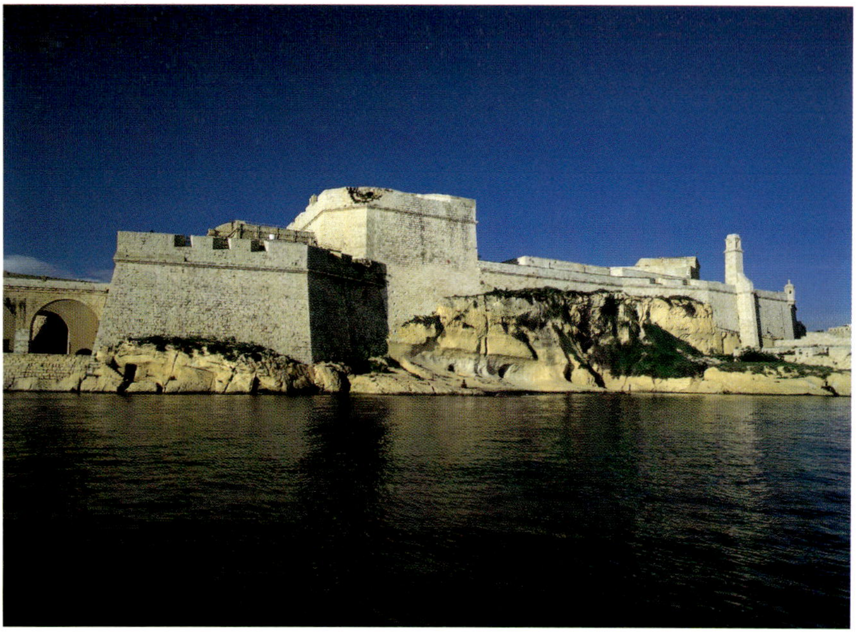

Fort St Angelo, Vittoriosa

Bontadino de Bontadini was harsher. They were sent into exile for two years following which they were deprived of the habit.

Caravaggio's flight by October 1608 remains to-date as mysterious as ever. He might have left the island on a vessel of one of the *padroni* documented in the 1690s who made frequent visits to the southern coast of Sicily and which might still have been active by this time. From among the noteworthy ones, Gabriele Russo and Giorgio Casanova often carried the correspondence of the Grand Master to various destinations. On one occasion, Gabriele Russo was also assigned the job of deporting a prisoner from Sicily to Malta but the hold of most *padroni* usually contained cargo of sorts. It is also worth noting that between 1564 and 1600, 18% of trips destined for Sicily arrived in Licata with the second largest number of trips arriving in Syracuse (15.6%).[26] It is therefore possible that Caravaggio did not choose his destination but simply left it to chance.

Willem Shellinks, *St Paul's Grotto* in the mid-17th century

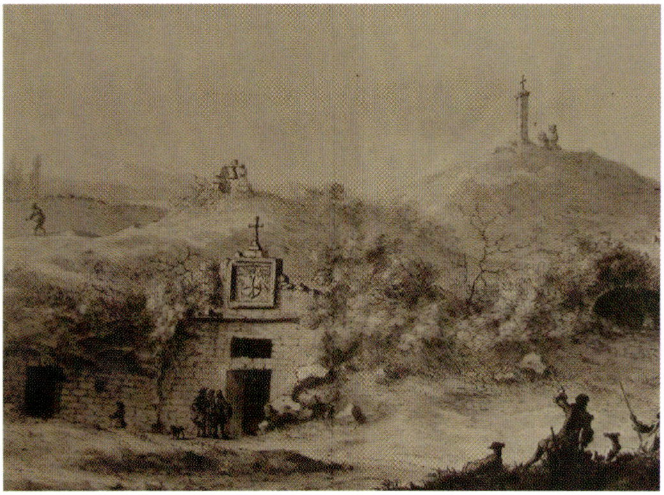

Religion and Identity

The cult of St Paul, the patron saint of Malta, witnessed a revival during the early 17th century and the Grotto of St Paul in Rabat soon became the centre of the local Pauline cult. The cult of St John and St Paul slowly began to be equated in favour of a more unified national identity. St Paul had brought Christianity to Malta but it was the Order of St John which had defended Malta against the Turks, and St John's severed head was impressed on local minted coinage as a symbol of the Order's authority. Wignacourt also built a chapel dedicated to St Paul which he built at St Paul's Bay where the saint was believed to have been shipwrecked. But Wignacourt's greatest achievement is perhaps the acquisition of St Paul's Grotto in 1617 with the subsequent foundation of a college. The Spanish hermit Juan Benegas de Cordoba was the main promoter of the revival of the Pauline cult. Thanks to his efforts and contacts, also made possible in part through Wignacourt's support, Benegas de Cordoba succeeded in acquiring relics from Rome and Sicily.[27] Benegas de Cordoba also had property and many acquaintances in Naples.

In February 1608, Fra Fabritio Sforza Colonna arrived in harbour from Palermo with a large reliquary holding numerous relics that the Spanish Viceroy in Sicily, the Marquis of Vilhena, had donated to Benegas de Cordoba. Amongst the witnesses to the attestation produced by Wignacourt the name of Fra Giacomo Marchese is again listed suggesting common acquaintances between Caravaggio and Benegas. The reliquary was taken to the Oratory of the former Conventual Church of St John's in April 1608 and a selection of relics extracted and placed in bust reliquaries commissioned earlier by Benegas in Naples. The box included relics of the apostles and other virgin saints and remained in the Oratory for months until finally taken in solemn procession to St Paul's Grotto. Caravaggio was then probably frequenting the Oratory as a novice, soon to be bestowed with a knighthood, and was soon to start working on his large canvas for the Oratory representing the beheading of St John the Baptist. The artist might have been familiar with this collection of reliquaries and busts but there is little to suggest that they caught his attention.

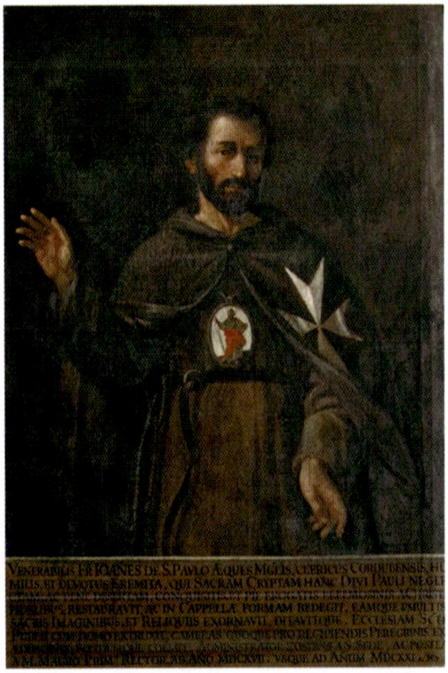

Fra Pietro Erardi, Juan Benegas de Cordoba, Rabat, Malta, Wignacourt Museum

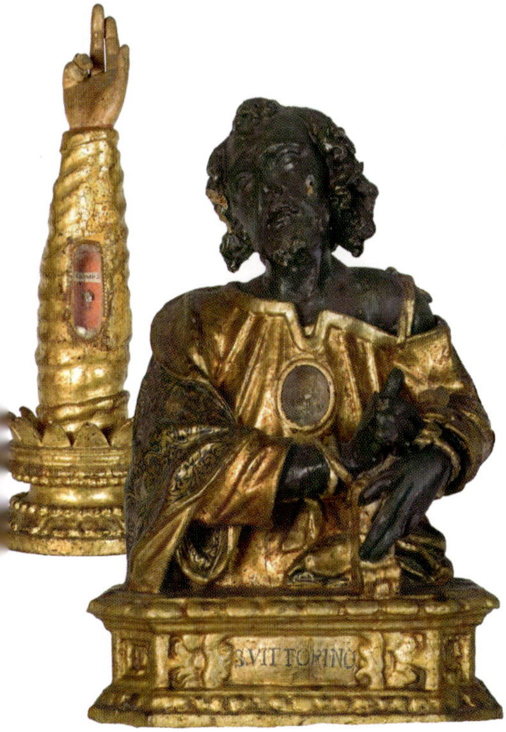

17th century reliquaries from St Paul's Grotto, Rabat, Malta

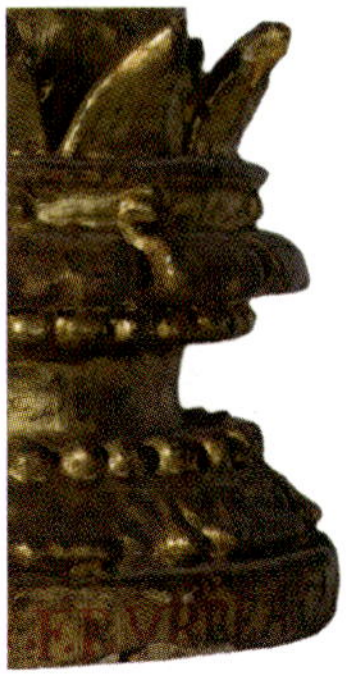

Detail of arm reliquary with commemorative inscription, St Paul's Grotto, Rabat, Malta

The Art of a Master on an Island

Caravaggio's paintings known or proposed as painted in Malta relate to a very close circle of knights. The painter did not produce anything for the local churches and parishes nor for the religious orders. Even lost paintings are generally documented in connection with private patronage and no local merchants or elites could acquire anything by his hand. Works by followers or emulators of Caravaggio's style were nonetheless in demand and had Caravaggio decided to stay in Malta, more commissions would have been forthcoming. But the quality of his two known works on the island surpasses that of any of his followers in both technique and content.

Caravaggio's *St Jerome* represents an aged saint sitting on his bed while writing on a table nearby. St Jerome strives to react in silence to a shaft of light that illuminates his torso and inspires his writings on which he concentrates his attention. It is the same light that brings the dead to life in Caravaggio's *Raising of Lazarus* and communicatively illuminates in his *Calling of Matthew* for the Contarelli Chapel at San Luigi dei Francesi (Rome). Jerome has risen from his sleep to list his ideas in a small notebook almost akin to an artists' sketch book lest he forgets by the morrow. It is a personal painting by Caravaggio who also included the crucifix and the penance stone which he omitted in his other representations of the saint. It is strikingly reminiscent of Ippolito Malaspina's personal vicissitudes who renounced his command of the papal fleet held since August 1603 to retire in solitude distributing his wealth to the poor.[28] This is much like St Jerome's renunciation of his status as a Roman prelate choosing instead a contemplative life in poverty. This evidence of religiosity so akin to Tridentine thought is achieved with the same stirring calmness as Caravaggio's larger public work representing the martyrdom of St John the Baptist. The event seems depicted for an audience but removed from the curious eyes of

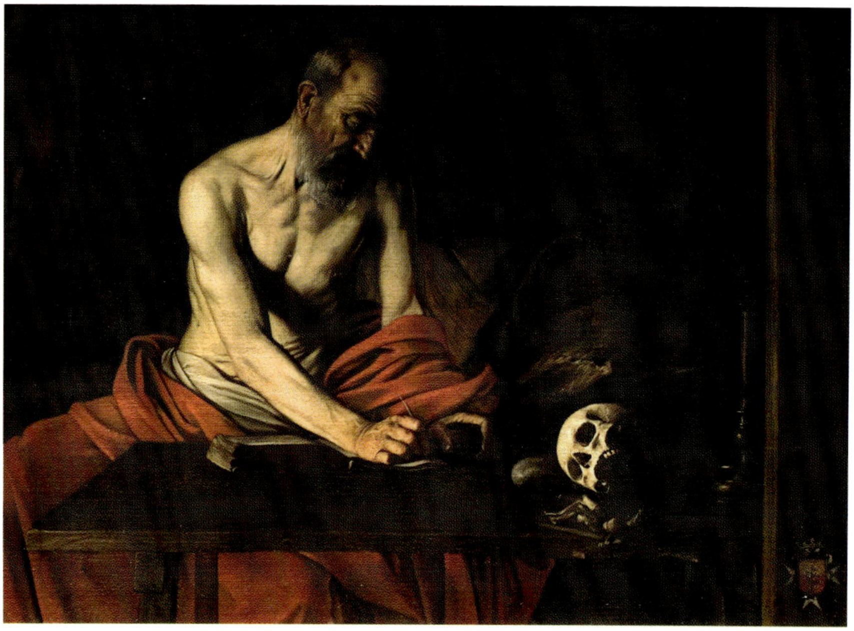

Caravaggio, *St Jerome*, Valletta, St John's Co-Cathedral

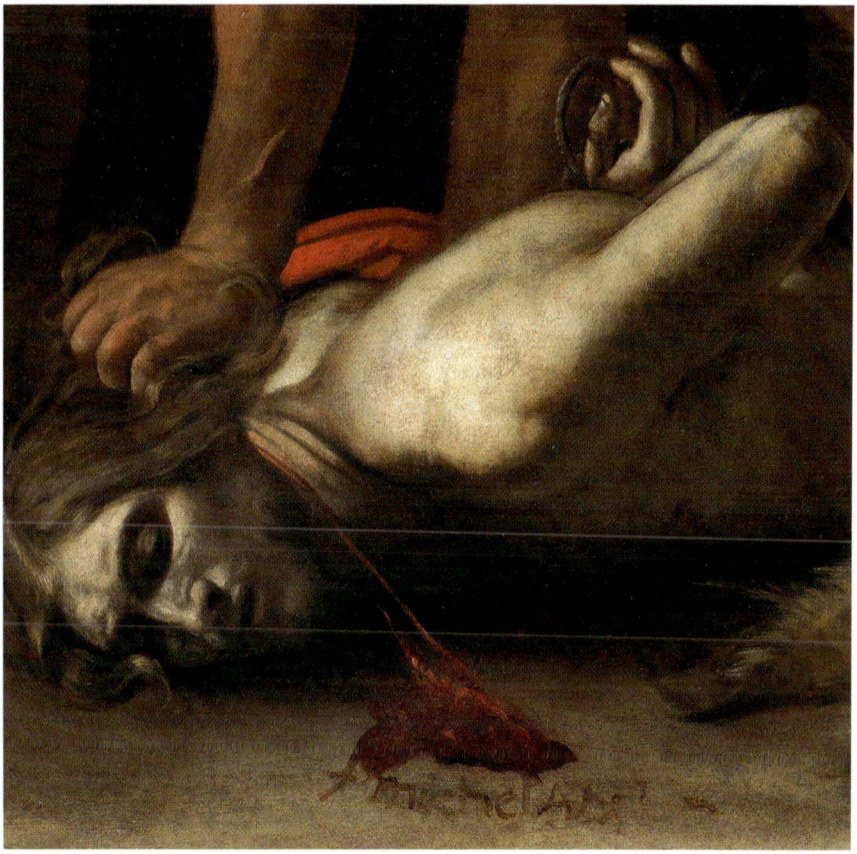

Detail of Caravaggio's *Beheading of St John the Baptist*, Valletta, St John's Co-Cathedral

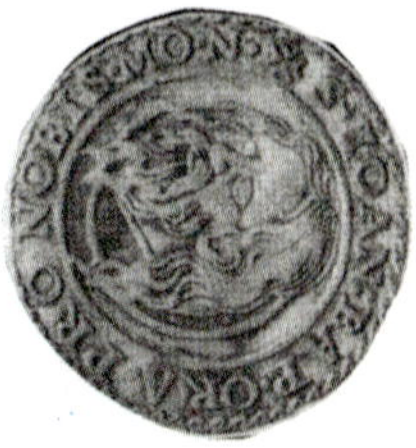

Coin from Wignacourt's magistracy featuring the severed head of the Baptist

the other prisoners. Yet it is the choice of the fleeting moment represented that is indeed significant. The crime has been committed; envy has been appeased and the prize for Salome's dance is about to be delivered. There is nothing that an onlooker can do as the head is being severed from the body following the beheading. Contemporaries might have chosen to represent the severed head being held high by the executioner. Others would have opted to represent the saint about to be beheaded. Caravaggio chose to represent in-between; the Baptist's head was soon to become a relic and representations were exhibited in churches for public devotion. There was nothing in Malta that could influence such a novel approach. His only signed canvas contrasts sharply with his *Seven Acts of Mercy*, a carefully balanced and complex composition, produced in Naples a few months earlier.

Caravaggio appears to have found himself comfortable in Malta. He could communicate with his peers and live in a cosmopolitan city that was not far off from other Italian cities. Peripheral Malta was no match to Rome but the island was no cultural backwater. Its strategic geographic location on the periphery of the Christian kingdoms made it an easy prey for Ottoman incursions but the Order did hit back with equal efficiency. Malta was to have its fist contribution in Maltese historiography within a few decades and her ever-growing economic well-being would soon translate into works of art and architecture for the local communities.

Images of the Divine

Caravaggio's followers and their art through a selection of paintings from Malta's national collection

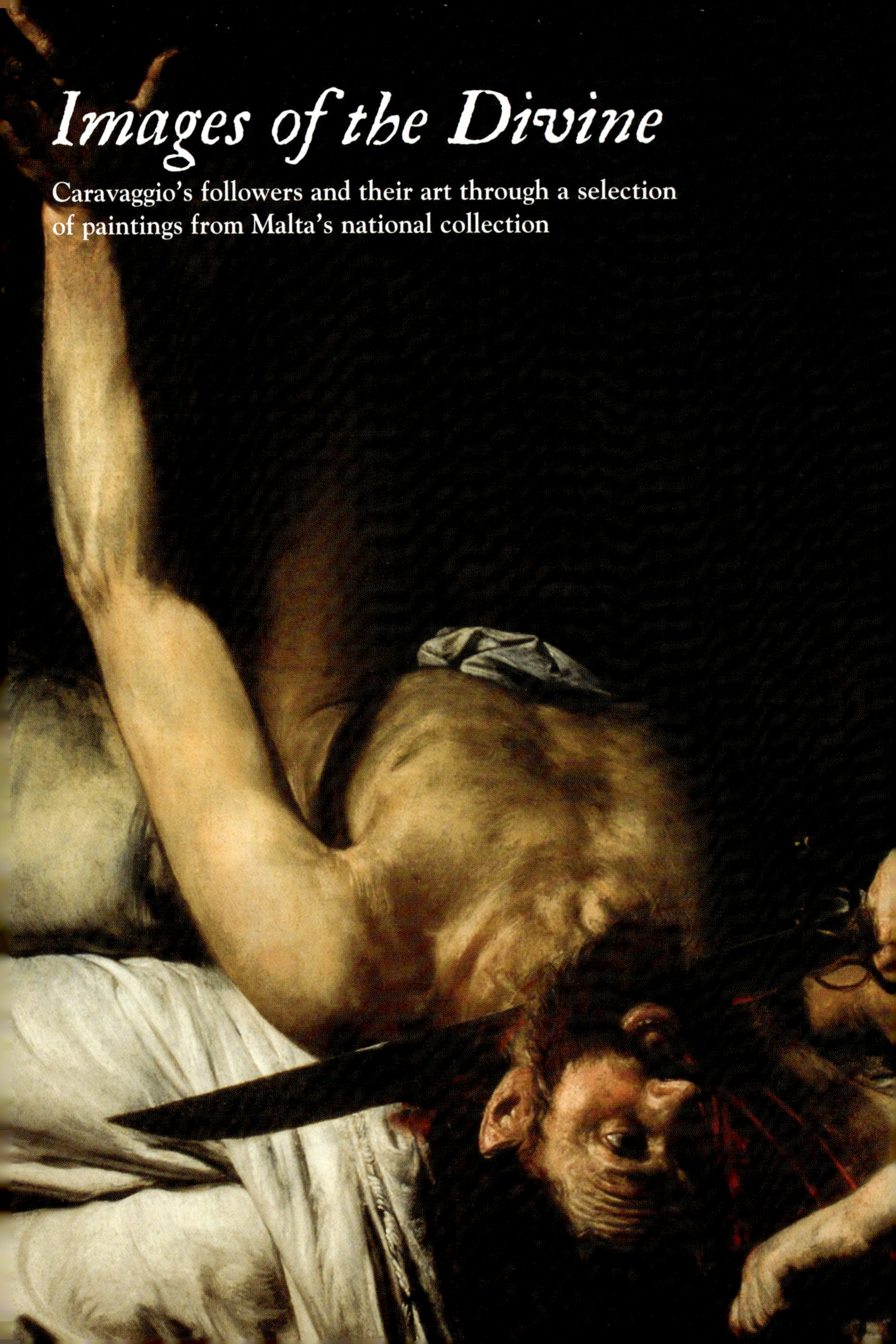

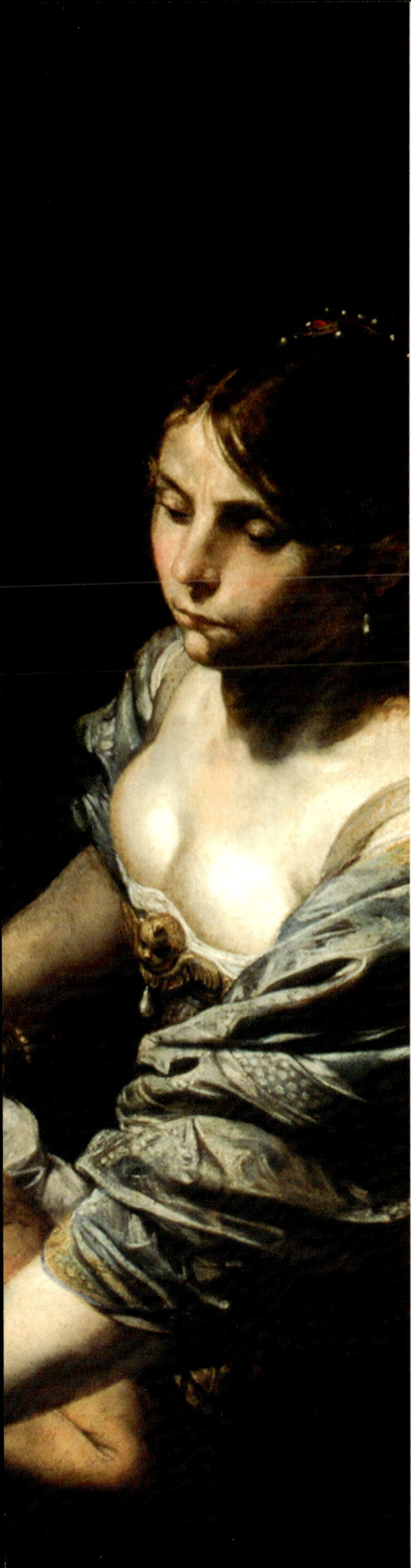

With his first public commissions in 1599 for the Contarelli Chapel in the church of San Luigi dei Francesi (Rome), Caravaggio's style and innovative approach to both painting and subject transformed him into the most famous painter in Rome. His paintings had an unprecedented novelty and immediately attracted attention. He had chosen his subjects from the lowly Roman taverns and renounced the imitation of antique marbles that contemporary artists practised. Michelangelo Buonarroti and Raphael meant little to Caravaggio in comparison to nature which he recognised as his master. Refraining from idealising his figures, Caravaggio seemingly painted in a dark room with a shaft of light aimed at giving force through contrast. The religious event begins to occur in the immediacy of contemporary life and as Caravaggio's Christ calls Matthew from amongst the rowdy revellers in the tavern, Caravaggio's art called young artists to this new revelation in art. Caravaggio did not accept followers and imitators but his style inspired artists working in Rome, Naples, Genoa and other European cities. Northern and French artists active in Rome also faithfully absorbed elements of his style and subject matter.[1]

Contemporaries in Rome

Two of Caravaggio's contemporaries, Giovanni Baglione (1573-1644) and Guido Reni (1575-1642), were indeed influenced by Caravaggio's innovative art but the works of both in the Maltese national collection are removed from Caravaggio's immediate impact. Baglione was amongst the first to absorb Caravaggio's style although he initially worked as a mannerist

La Valentin, *Judith and Holofernes*, Valletta, National Museum of Fine Arts

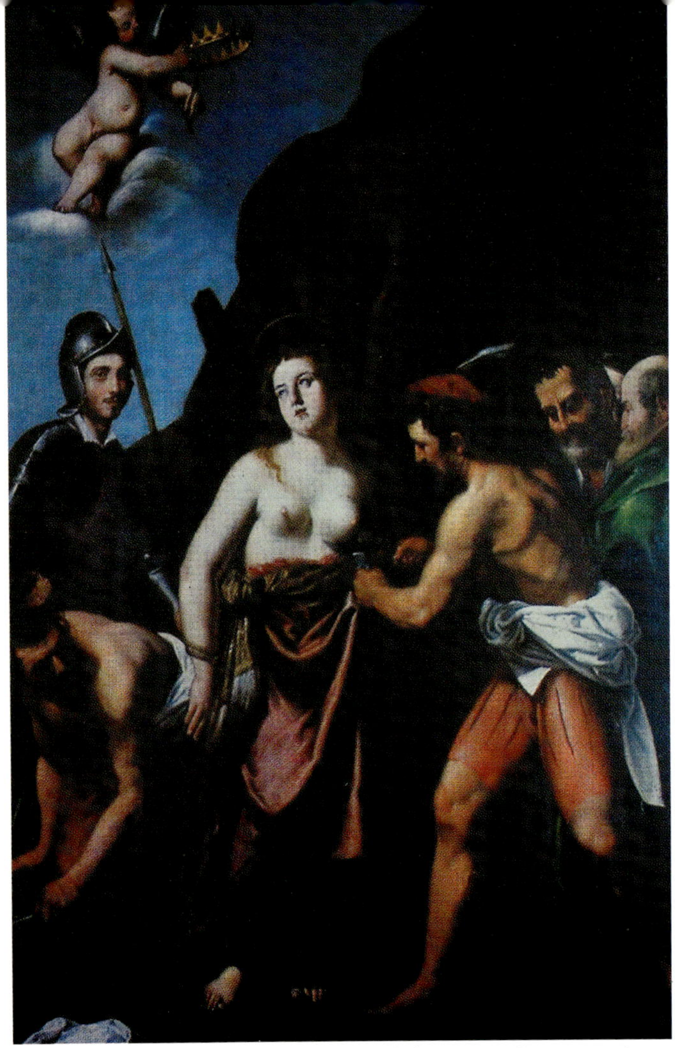

Giovanni Baglione, *Martyrdom of St Agatha*, Valletta, Museum of Fine Arts

Guido Reni's, *Triumph of Samson*, Bologna, Pinacoteca Nazionale

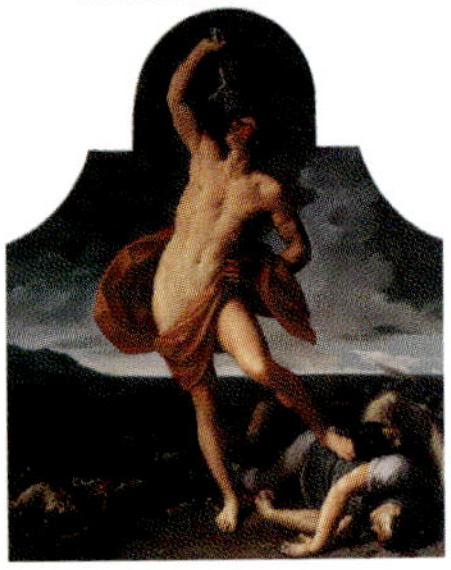

painter. He did criticise Caravaggio's art and its inability to conceive aesthetic beauty and is best remembered for the court case he instituted in 1603 against Caravaggio and his friends for disseminating libellous writings against him. Baglione's two versions representing *Divine Love overcoming the World, the Flesh and the Devil* (Staatliche Museen zu Berlin; Galleria Nazionale d'Arte Antica, Rome) painted in 1602 best summarises his compromising approach to Caravaggio's naturalism which he tempers with idealisations.

In Baglione's attributed *Martyrdom of St Agatha* in the Maltese national collection the main action revolves around the saint, standing at the centre of the composition, about to be martyred by having her breasts cut off by two executioners. A youthful soldier looks beyond the canvas onto the onlooker, suggesting a self-portrait. Two men are engaged in conversation on the happening while an angel hovers above holding a palm frond and the crown of martyrdom. In a similar manner to his writings on art, Baglione included idealisations in his figures and is not directly in touch with Caravaggio's naturalism. The painting was acquired by the Gollcher foundation for the National Museum of Fine Arts in 1967.

The Bolognese Guido Reni was to foster an interest in Caravaggio's style during the first decade of the 17th century when he was living in Rome. Reni was an aristocratic yet meditative painter who absorbed classical culture through Raffaello Sanzio's works and his interest in antique marbles. He was trained in Bologna with Annibale Carracci (1560-1609) then working in a style that recreates nature through classical and Renaissance art. His interest in Caravaggio's art is best represented by two works, namely his *Crucifixion of St Peter* (Vatican collection, Rome) and his *David with the Head of Goliath* (Louvre, Paris). The *Crucifixion of St Peter* is a reworking of Caravaggio's original composition for the Cerasi Chapel at the church of Santa Maria del Popolo (Rome) whilst his *David and Goliath* re-interprets Caravaggio's style almost suggesting plagiarism.

Reni's *Christ holding the Cross* in Malta's national collection has been recently dated to c.1620. The figure of Christ inspired from Michelangelo Buonarroti's *Risen Christ* (Santa Maria Sopra Minerva, Rome) stands holding the cross within a solitary landscape. The painting was imported to Malta during Grand Master Alof de Wignacourt's

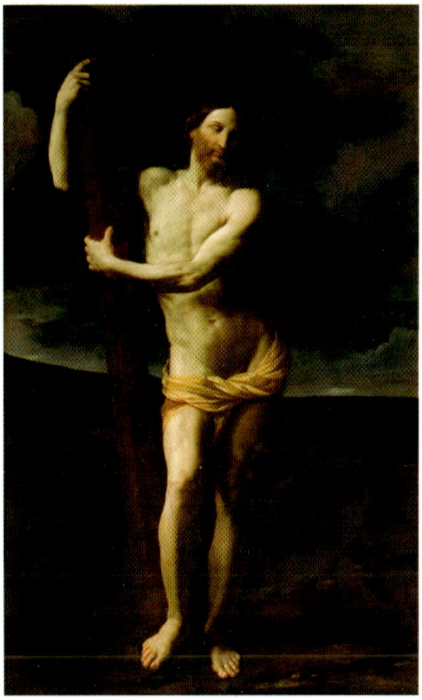

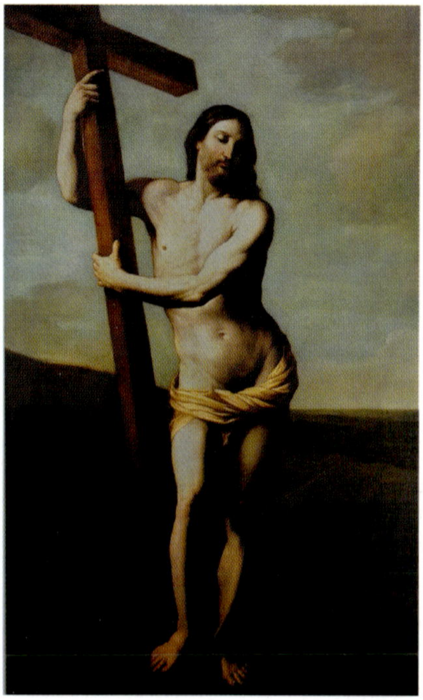

Left: Guido Reni, *Christ holding the Cross*, Valletta, Museum of Fine Arts

Right: Madrid's version of Reni's *Christ holding the Cross*

magistracy and hung in the Grand Master's palace. It does suggest common points with Reni's contemporary *Atlanta and Hippomenes* (Louvre, Paris) but the placement of a lone figure in a solitary landscape is perhaps more reminiscent of Reni's *Triumph of Samson* (Pinacoteca Nazionale di Bologna). This latter similarity might suggests the possibility of a slightly earlier date. An almost contemporary version by Reni belongs to the Museum of the Real Academia de San Fernando in Madrid dated slightly later to 1621.[2] Numerous copies of Reni's *Christ holding the Cross* were produced during the following decades; a further version as yet unidentified after Reni was in store at the Grand Master's Palace in Valletta during the early 19th century.

Caravaggisti in Rome

Caravaggio had neither a school nor an organised workshop where followers and apprentices could absorb and learn his art. No direct follower could take Caravaggio's place after his sudden departure from Rome in 1606. Perhaps only Bartolomeo Manfredi (1587-1620) provided this continuity by taking up Caravaggio's quest for naturalism.[3] Manfredi's canvases have a greater accent on subject matter focusing mainly on genre related scenes. They are indeed more refined than Caravaggio's. Manfredi did not manage to attract large-scale public commissions and his art remained restricted to private patronage mainly acquired for domestic interiors. Manfredi's particular approach to Caravaggio did however influence a number of painters active in Rome foremost amongst whom Valentin de Boulogne (1591-1632).[4] Born in Columniers, Le Valentin's early presence in Rome is still unknown but by the late 1620s he established himself in the city also thanks to the patronage of the Barberini family. His major commission is the altar painting of *St Processus and Martinian* for St Peter's

Michelangelo's Buonarotti's *Risen Christ*, Rome, Sta Maria Sopra Minerva

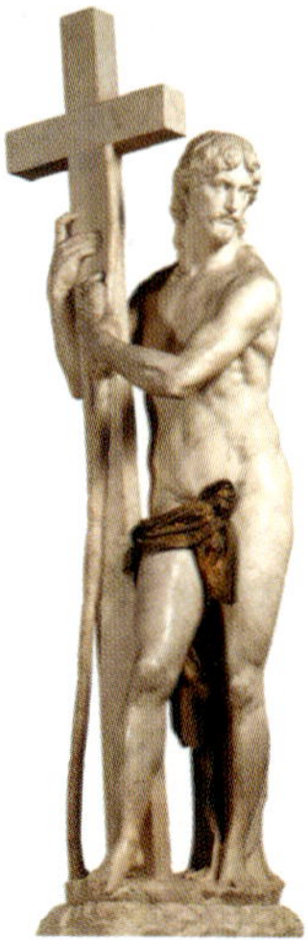

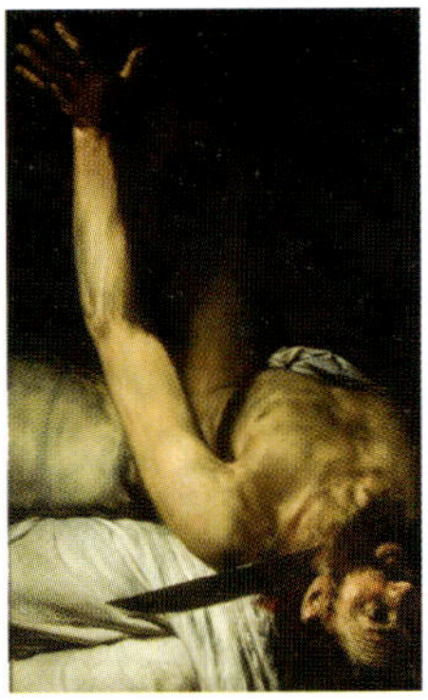

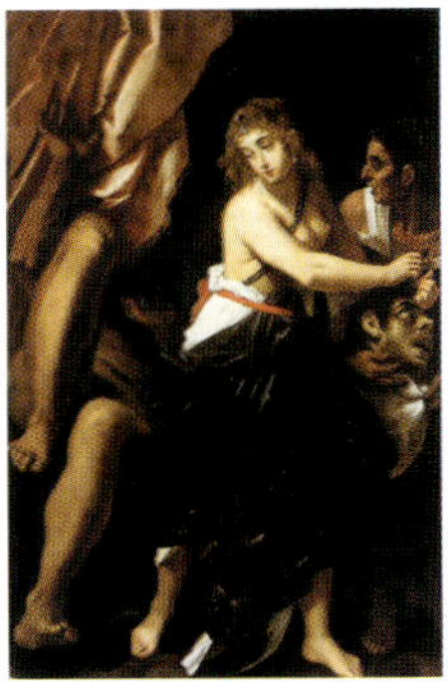

Above: Details from Le Valentin's (top) and Baglione's *Judith and Holofernes*, Rome, Galleria Borghese

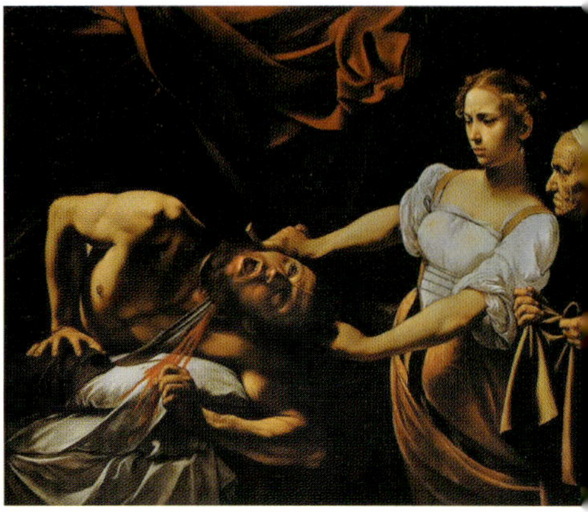

Above right: Caravaggio, *Judith and Holofernes*, Rome, Gallaria Nazionale d'Arte Antica

Basilica in Rome but his works also take up the subject matter popularized by Manfredi.

Le Valentin's *Judith and Holofernes* depicts Judith, dressed in 17th century fashion and costume, as the maiden of the lord who moves in resolute determination to sever Holofernes' head. Judith is bathed in a strong side-light symbolical of the divine that guides her hand; she is indeed the bringer of death through which liberty and a new life are won for the Israelites. It is the very divine-natured light that the agonized Holofernes seeks to hide in vain solely by his hand. Indeed a suggested deeper reading has much to do with the concept of deception on being deceived which is also in line with Le Valentin's genre paintings inspired by Caravaggio and Manfredi. Dateable to 1623, Le Valentin's *Judith and Holofernes* is stylistically a first attempt by the artist to shift away from Manfredi's style. The interpretation of subject matter by Le Valentin in his *Judith and Holofernes* suggests a direct inspiration from Caravaggio's own version but Le Valentin's work depicts the happening from a high viewpoint in contrast to Caravaggio's frontal immediacy. In spite of Caravaggio's influence on Le Valentin, particular details such as the combination of raised and lowered foot in the figure of Holofernes are reminiscent of Baglione's treatment of the same subject in his 1608 *Judith and Holofernes* (Galleria Borghese, Rome). Le Valentin's *Judith and Holofernes* was purchased from an Italian collection in 1926 through the efforts of the former Curator of Fine Arts, Vincenzo Bonello.

Northern Caravaggisti – the case of Mathias Stomer

Although considered a French Caravaggista, Le Valentin interacted very well with a group of Dutch artists from Utrecht whose major exponents are generally identified as Gerrit van Honthorst (1590-1656) also known as Gerardo delle Notti, Dirck van

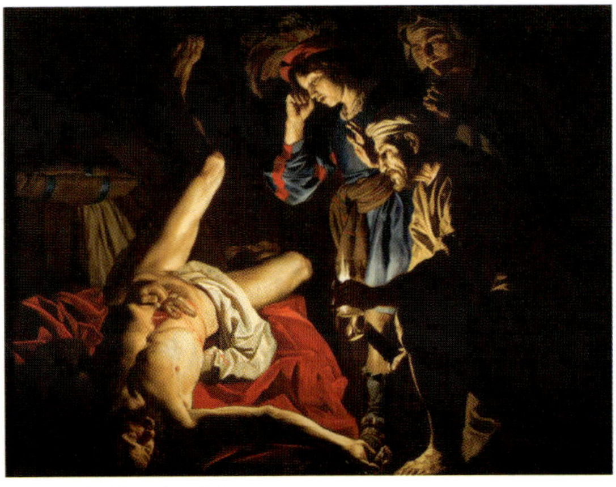

Stomer's *Death of Cato*

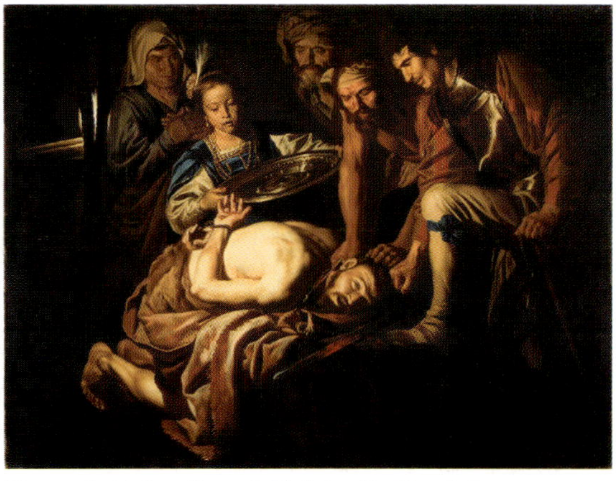

Stomer's *Beheading of St John the Baptist*

Baburen (1595-1624), and Hendrick Terbrugghen (1588-1629). This group of Northern artists represents an innovative approach to Caravaggio's art mainly related to their manipulative application of light, oftentimes included in the picture, through a device first suggested by the Italian painter Carlo Saraceni (1580-1620).[5]

An artist whose works in the national collection best represents this innovative application of Caravaggio's style is Mathias Stomer (c.1600-c.1650).[6] The earliest biographical reference to Stomer is dateable to 1630-32 and records *Matteo Stom[er], fiamengo pittore, di anni 30* (Mathias Stom[er], Flemish painter, thirty years old) then living in the parish of San Nicola in Arcione, Rome. Around 1632 he moved to Naples but was in Sicily by the end of the decade where he was mainly active in Palermo and Messina until his death. The chronology of his paintings has been established largely on the basis of their internal evidence but his art remains elusive. Stomer's stylistic vocabulary, learned initially from the Northern followers of Caravaggio and then experienced first-hand in Rome, was further enhanced by Stomer's access to the later works of Caravaggio in Naples and Rome.

The four paintings by Stomer in our national collection represent two different trends of Caravaggism. In his *Lamentation over the Dead Abel* and the biblical subject generally identified as *The Good Samaritan*, Stomer manipulates light, which he introduces into the canvas through diagonal shafts, to model his figures and highlight the dramatic subject represented. In his *Death of Cato* and his *Beheading of St John* Stomer utilized a source of light within the painting to enhance the inherent drama of the subject. These differing choices might suggest different dates for each of these works. Stomer is closest in concept to Gerrit van Honthorst in those canvases where he utilized internal lighting but he is more Italianate and a more markedly pronounced follower of Caravaggio's art in his paintings that utilize diagonal lighting. Stomer's canvases were presented to our national collection in 1929. by Comm. Augusto Lurati of San Remo (Italy) in lieu of excise duty.

The *Lamentation over the Dead Abel* describes the end result of the biblical fratricide between Cain and Abel. The figure of Eve, partially obstructed from vision by an emotive Adam and the dead body of their son, is represented in its human fragility. Indeed Stomer's

Battistello Carracciolo, *Lamentation over the dead Abel*, Naples, Capodimonte Museum

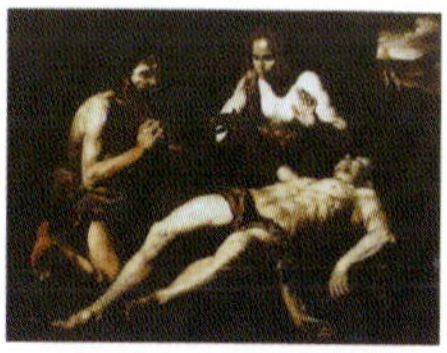

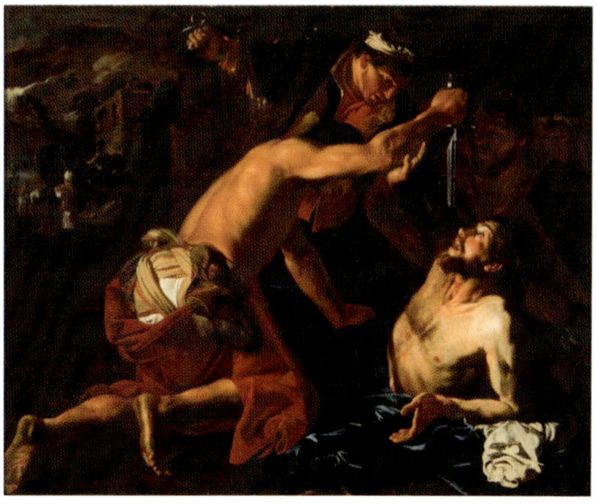

Stomer's *The Good Samaritan*

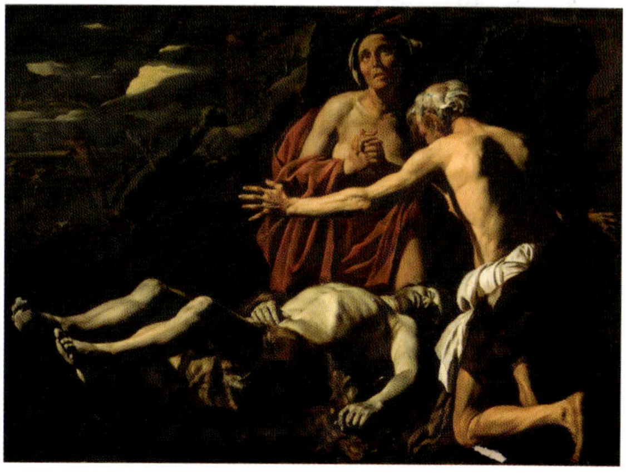

Stomer's *Lamentation over the dead Abel*

Eve prefigures the Virgin of Sorrows through her upward stance and joined hands suggesting prayer and resolute acceptance of the plight of her son. This work might have been inspired directly from Caravaggio's style and interesting similarities in composition can be proposed with a painting of the same subject by the Neapolitan artist Battistello Caracciolo (Capodimonte Museum, Naples). Stomer's *Good Samaritan* represents a man being assaulted by thieves. The commotion happening close to the picture plane is ignored by the Samaritan who walks away unheadingly in the background. Stomer adopts a similar compositional device to the one used for his *Lamentation over the Dead Abel* where the action in the background is an extension of the happening in the foreground. The facial type of the victim assaulted by thieves also recalls that the facial type of Stomer's *Prometheus* (private collection, Rome). In Stomer's *Death of Cato*, the philosopher, with his entrails spurting out of his chest, lies down on a bright red mattress-cover attended by an emotive young man and an elderly couple. All three are identified by Plutarch, the author of the classical narrative about Cato, as members of Cato's household who discover the suicide during the night. This painting could be one of Stomer's Sicilian works where his style became rather hard-edged and almost mechanical. It might also be the one purchased directly from the artist by the Sicilian Antonio Ruffo around 1646-1649. A painting of the same subject having a strikingly similar composition is at the Pinacoteca Civica (Cento, Italy). Stomer's *Martyrdom of St John the Baptist* indeed strikes an interesting comparison with Caravaggio's own version in the Oratory of the former Conventual Church of St John's. A closely-knit group assists to the beheading of St John the Baptist. The saint is already dead and his head about to be completely severed from his body with a knife, much like Caravaggio's very own Maltese version. The penetrating gaze of the severed head of the Baptist who stands diagonally and close to the picture plane entices the onlooker. He is in sharp contrast to the executioner and the accompanying spectators who all focus on the action whilst a richly dressed girl holding a silver charger is expecting to collect the severed head.

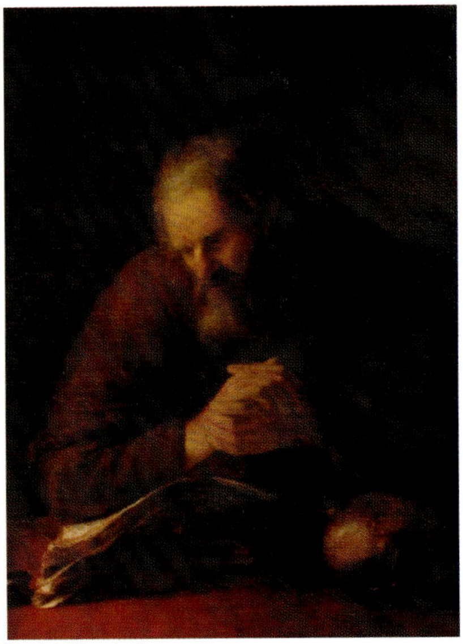

17th century Dutch School, *St Jerome*, Valletta, National Museum of Fine Arts

A further painting stylistically attributable to the 17th century Dutch school (1646?) provides an interesting comparison to Caravaggio's other paintings representing *St Jerome* (Galleria Borghese, Rome; St. John's Co-Cathedral, Valletta). The saint is represented frontally and close to the picture plane with clasped hands fully absorbed in reading an open book. A skull and an inkpot are included on the table and the close angle through which the saint is portrayed suggests an intimate setting. The author of this painting has remained elusive although a possible monogram inscribed within a circular geometric shape could be indicative of

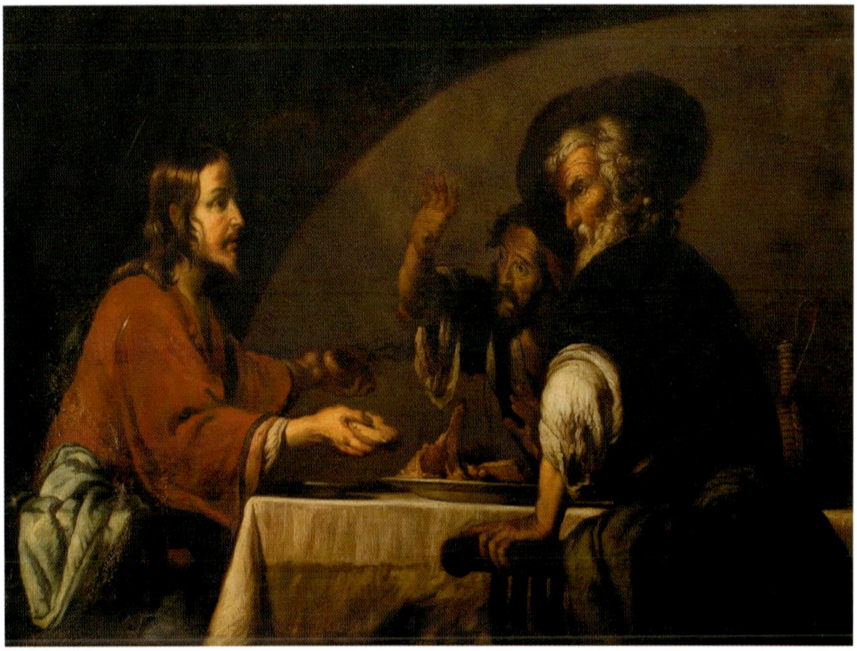

Bernardo Strozzi(?), *Supper at Emmaus*, Valletta, Grand Master's Palace

the artist. Its softer chromatic qualities suggest a Dutch artist whose art bears evidence to Caravaggio's impact on Dutch 17th century painting. The painting was orginally in the Grand Master's Palace collection.

A possible Genoese Connection

Particular inventories of the palace refer to a *Supper at Emmaus* identified as a work of the Flemish 17th century school. The painting is probably the same one included by Brockdorff in his representation of one of the halls of the Grand Master's Palace dateable to the early 19th century and can be securely identified with a painting currently located in the Grand Master's Palace in Valletta. In the late 19th century, Linntorn Simmons described the subject of this painting as 'The Supper at Emmaus – Our Lord seated; the two disciples rising. The heads are said to be portraits of unknown persons.' The same author also mentions a second painting of the same subject which he identified as a work of one of Preti's assistants. The surviving painting describes the meeting of two of Christ's followers with their master after the resurrection. Christ sits at the end of a table with his two followers sitting opposite. They

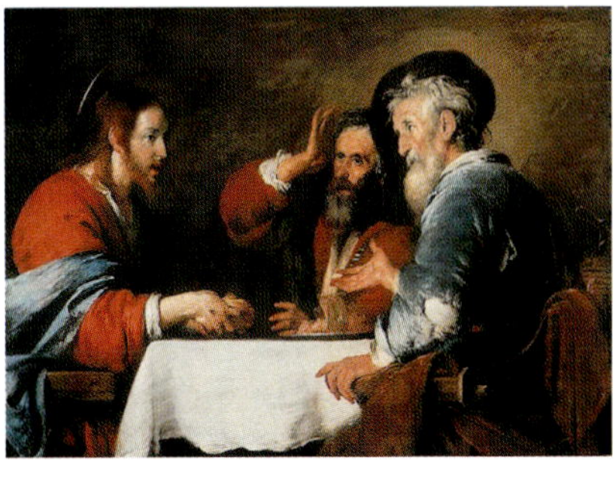

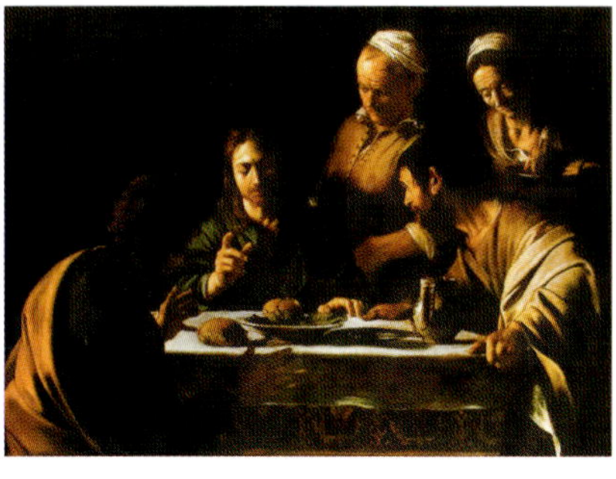

Left: Bernardo Strozzi's *Supper at Emmaus*, Grenoble, Musée de Grenoble

Right: Caravaggio's *Supper at Emmais*, Milan, Brera

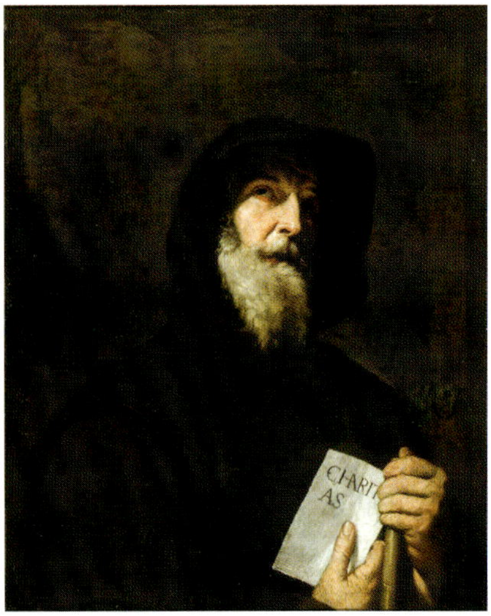

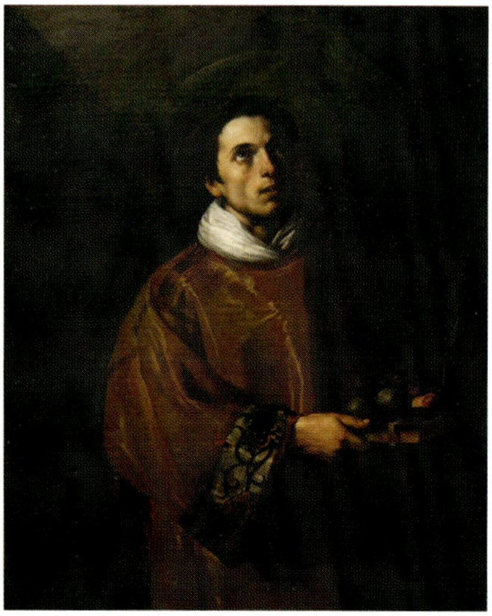

Left: Attributed to Jusepe Ribera, *St Stephen,* Valletta, National Museum of Fine Arts

Right: Jusepe Ribera, *St Francis of Paola,* Valletta, National Museum of Fine Arts

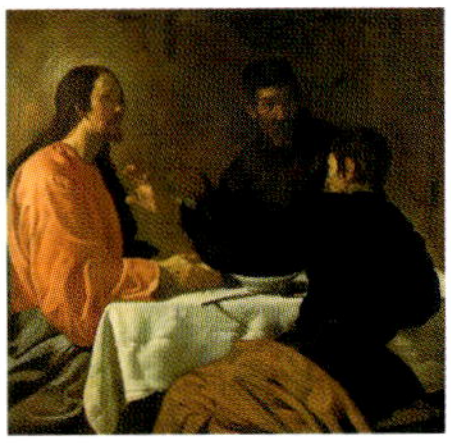

Diego Velazquez, *Supper at Emmaus*, New York, Metropolitan Museum of Art

are caught by surprise at the sudden revelation of their companion's identity as he, Christ, breaks the bread in two. The older man wearing a distinctive hat and sitting with his back to the picture plane seems to rise from the Savonarola chair he is sitting on while his companion, arms raised, bends forward as if to confirm the true identity of their companion, Christ.

Depictions of Caravaggio's *Supper at Emmaus* are not exclusive to Caravaggio's famous two versions (National Gallery, London and Pinacoteca di Brera, Milan). Earlier versions of the same subject were produced by Giacobo Bassano (1515-1592), Jacobo Pontormo (1494-1557) and Giacobo Robusti known as Tintoretto (1518-1594) among others. Bassano's version, also contextualized within the Lombard school from which Caravaggio was to come forward, is perhaps the closest to Caravaggio's two versions but the subject was also taken up by the generation of artists following Caravaggio such as Diego Velazquez (1599-1660).

Jusepe Ribera, *St Francis of Paola*, detail

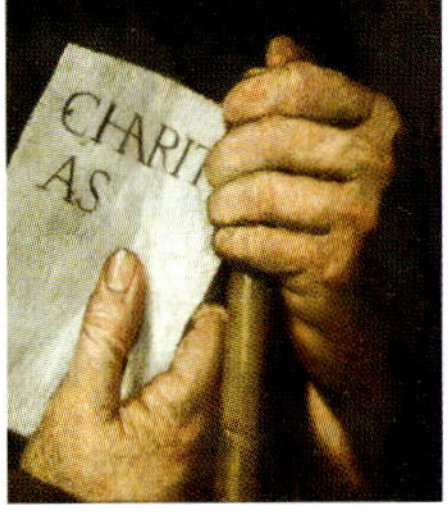

Details from this painting suggest striking similarities with the works of the Genoese painter Bernardo Strozzi (1581-1644). The subject matter of the *Supper at Emmaus* is strikingly similar in composition to Strozzi's version (Grenoble Museum of Art, France) dateable to the second quarter of the 17th century when Strozzi had by then moved to Venice. The Grenoble version is also stylistically reminiscent of northern European art; by the 1620s the Genoese were fostering a taste for such art. A working drawing representing the head of a man by Strozzi (Louvre, Paris) can possibly also be identified with the figure of the apostle in the background raising his hand in amazement at the revelation of Christ. A second drawing (Louvre) reworks the head of the apostle wearing a large hat who rises in surprise at the revelation.

Strozzi, also known as 'Il Capuccino', was a Genoese painter who had joined the Capuchin Order while still in his teens; hence his nickname. In 1610 he left the convent but continued working as a painter, leaving for Venice by 1630. Works by Strozzi in the Maltese national collection include a *Portrait of an Unidentified Lady* attributed to the artist by the Italian art historian Roberto Longhi in 1929 on being then acquired from the collection of the Bellanti family.[7] The Venetian painterly qualities of this portrait suggest a date within Strozzi's Venetian sojourn. A second painting attributed to Strozzi by the late Dr John Cauchi, former curator of fine arts, represents the expulsion of Adam and Eve from the Garden of Eden and is now at the Cathedral Museum in Mdina. The painting indeed has a historical provenance that confirms the presence of works by Strozzi in Malta at least during the late 18th and early 19th century if not before.[8]

The Neapolitan Caravaggisti

Caravaggio's short stays in Naples in 1607 and 1609 left a marked impact on the artistic environment of the city. The major exponent to immediately draw from Caravaggio's style was Battistello Caracciolo, a Neapolitan artist originally trained in the Mannerist style but who converted to Caravaggism following Caravaggio's stay in the city. By the 1620s the major exponents of Caravaggio's style in Naples can be identified in the Valencian artist Jusepe Ribera also known as Lo Spagnoletto (1595-1652) and Massimo Stanzione (1585-1656). The latter remains initially Caravaggesque in spirit and style but his art slowly drifted away into a classicizing trait. Ribera retained his popular approach to Caravaggism and its inherent naturalism still identifying his saints and heroes from the common people. Caravaggio's style managed to acquire a firm foothold in Naples, yet some canvases remain to date unascribed and with equivocal titles. Such is the case of a portrait, tentatively ascribed to the 17th century Neapolitan school, representing a bearded man with a pensive gesture occasionally identified as *Heraclitus*, *St Peter* or *Man in Meditation*. The figure emerges from a dark background with a strong sidelight modelling the expressiveness of the bearded face.

In the Maltese national collection, Ribera is represented by a *St Francis of Paola*; an Italian saint from the region of Calabria and founder of the Hermits of St Francis of Assisi also known as the Minim Friars. In this painting, originally in the Grand Master's Palace

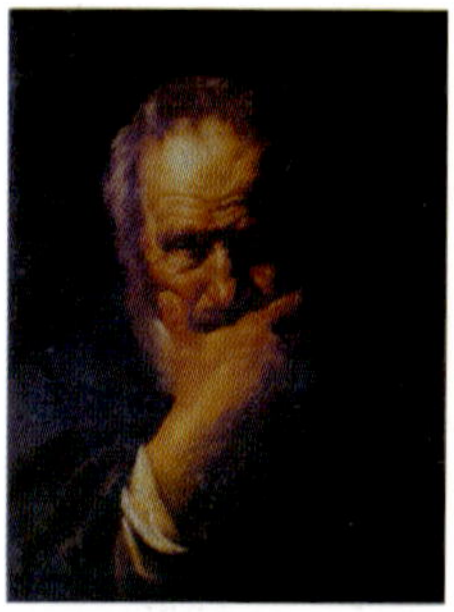

17th century Neapolitan school *Heraclitus*(?), Valletta, National Museum of Fine Arts

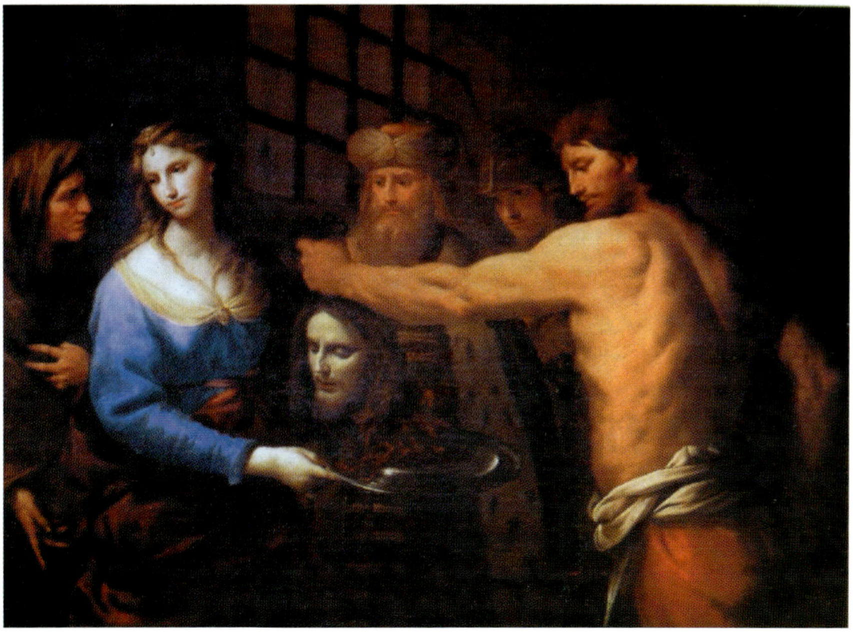

Andrea Vaccaro, *Salome receiving the Head of the Baptist*, Valletta, National Museum of Fine Arts

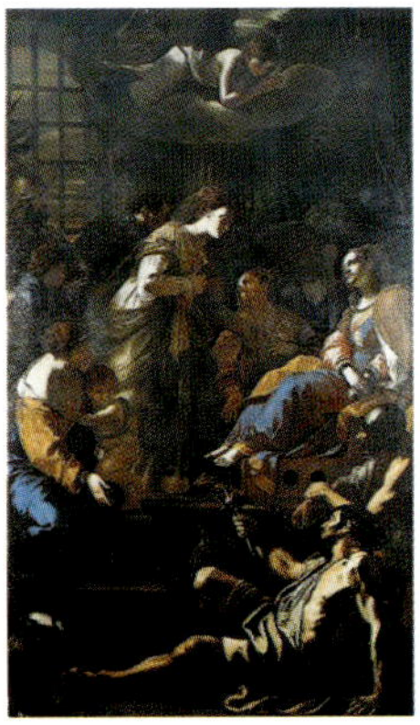

Mattia Preti, *St Catherine in Prison*, Ohio, Daytona Art Institute

collection, the saint looks up as he holds his staff and a paper inscribed – charitas in his hands. This is a very intimate painting focusing on the saint's face, almost suggesting a picture intended for a personal devotion. The quality of the piece does not deter from ascribing it to the master's hand. Three autograph versions are known but the prototype has been generally identified with a version in a private collection dateable to 1640.[9] The popularity of this painting is also confirmed by numerous copies in museums and other collections. A second painting representing *St Stephen* has also been attributed to Ribera and a *St Lawrence*, dressed in a similarly styled dalmatic, could possibly be related to second work attributed to Ribera. Born in Jativa (Valencia, Spain), Ribera went to Rome at an early age where he enrolled in the Accademia di San Luca but was mainly in contact with the northern Caravaggisti. In 1616 he moved to Naples where he was to remain active until his death. In Naples his art was mainly concerned with a crude realism.

A second Neapolitan painter much influenced by Massimo Stanzione is Andrea Vaccaro (1598-1670). Vaccaro's initial training was mainly as a Mannerist artist but by the 1620s had absorbed Caravaggio's art and was also copying such works as Caravaggio's *Flagellation of Christ* (Capodimonte Museum, Naples).[10] By the following decade Vaccaro was closer to the art of Guido Reni and other contemporaries of whom he made copies for Neapolitan collectors and dealers. The works closest to Caravaggio's style, being also his earliest are his *David with the Head of Goliath* (Fondazione Longhi, Florence) and *St Sebastian* (Naples, Capodimonte). Vaccaro's *Salome Receiving the Head of the Baptist* depicts an executioner handing the Baptist's severed head to Salome onto a silver salver which she holds in her hand. Salome seems uninvolved by the gesture opting to discourse instead with her maid-of-honour while Herod looks impassively at the happening. The painting is removed from Caravaggio's immediate naturalism and the effective use of light is mainly achieved through the artist's choice to set the scene within a prison environment. The painting was purchased from the Hazlitt Gallery of London in 1956 with Funds from the O.F. Gollcher Foundation.

Mattia Preti – the last of the Caravaggisti

The last of the Caravaggisti can perhaps be identified in Mattia Preti (1613-1699). Preti arrived in Rome around 1630 and remained in the city until 1644. He must have travelled widely and visited Venice, Parma and Bologna amongst other cities. Preti's earliest connection with Malta dates to 1642 when was made a knight of Magisterial Obedience by Pope Urban VIII. Following his stay in Naples where he was already commissioned canvases for the then Conventual Church of St John's, Preti came to Malta lured by

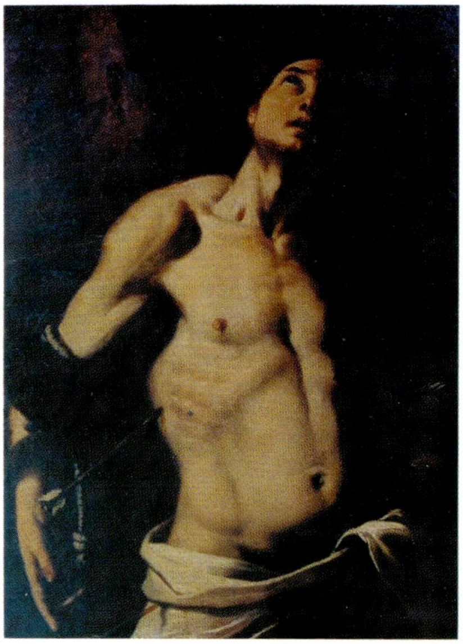

Mattia Preti, *St Sebastian*, Valletta, National Museum of Fine Arts

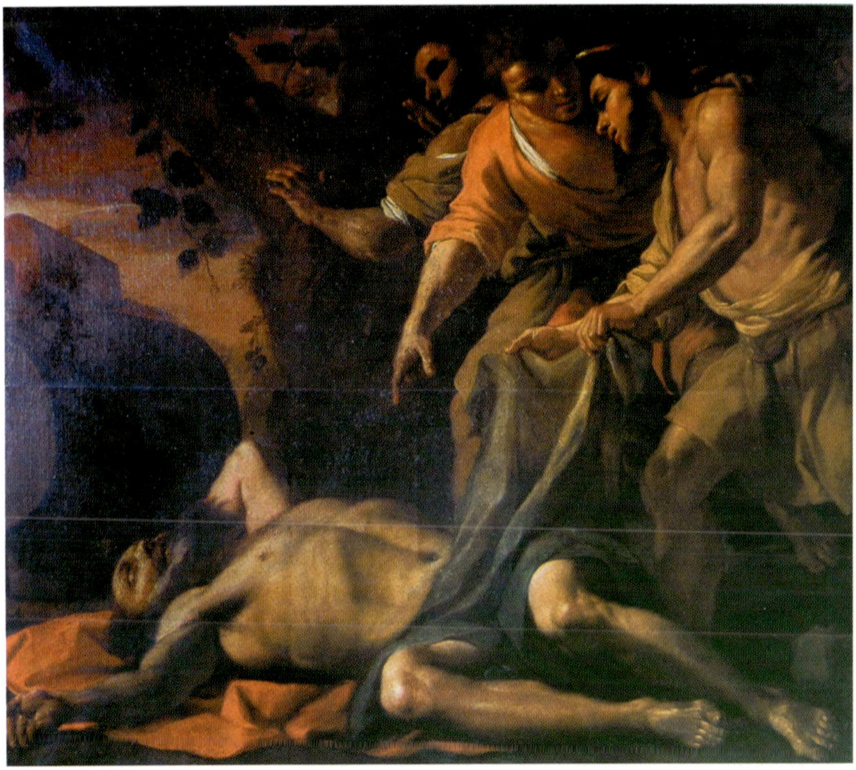

Mattia Preti, *Drunkeness of Noah*, Valletta, National Museum of Fine Arts

the prospect of becoming a Knight of Magisterial Grace which he achieved against the decoration of the entire vault of the then Conventual church. His work was not strictly related to the Order of St John but was also acquired and valued by local communities, lay confraternities and a wider spectrum of private patrons.

While in Rome, Preti came in contact with Caravaggio's style. There he could observe Caravaggio's art from close quarters and became attracted to subjects previously explored by Caravaggio's closest follower Manfredi. Preti however never utilised the outright representation of tavern life but instead focused mainly on penetrative and psychological interpretations. Indeed, Preti's interest in Caravaggio's art suggests that Caravaggism had the potential to continue well beyond the premature death of Valentin de Boulogne considered to be the last exponent of Caravaggio's art in Rome. Caravaggesque paintings by Preti from this period include his *St Catherine of Alexandria in Prison Visited by the Empress Faustina* (Art Institute, Dayton, Ohio) and the *Crucifixion of St Peter* (Musee de Pinture et Sculture, Grenoble). The Maltese national collection includes an exceptional group of Preti canvases produced during his Maltese sojourn when the artist had achieved an undisputed artistic maturity.His style had than matured following the influences of Guercino (1591-1666) and Lanfranco (1582-1647) and his art had also developed thanks to the influence of Venetian art. Preti's works in the national collection where mainly collected in the government hospital, the churches of the Order of St John and the Grand Master's Palace collection. These include his *Drunkeness of Noah, Lot and his Daughters* and his *Judith showing the head of Holofernes to the Bethulians*.

Preti's *St Sebastian* is perhaps the most striking representation of his interest in Caravaggio's art. Documented as painted in 1694, this painting is worked out in contrasting modelling of light and dark surfaces. Indeed, this canvas suggests Preti's interest in Caravaggio's art even towards the end of his life. The saint, tied to a tree trunk, looks upwards in resolute acceptance of his plight seemingly indifferent to the pain caused by the arrows shot at his torso. The painting belonged to the Prior of the Order Fra Pietro Viani whose seal is included on the back of the canvas. Preti's *Flagellation* and his *Crucifixion* dateable to 1683 also suggest the artist's interest in the style of Caravaggio.

Caravaggio's style and its interactions

The early 17th century did not exclusively witness Caravaggio's art and its quest for the representation of nature. Indeed, Caravaggio's art oftentimes interacted with the art of Annibale Carracci whose naturalism is amended to conform to the ideal. Although Caravaggio worked directly from life, he oftentimes recreated nature through contrived poses and gestures particularly during the last phase following his departure from Rome. In a sense, Caravaggio and Annibale Carracci are stylistically not far from each other. Caravaggio's art did not have an exclusive influence on his followers and many would absorb stylistic traits originating from both artists.

Caravaggio, *Martyrdom of St Matthew*, Rome, Church of San Luigi dei Francesi

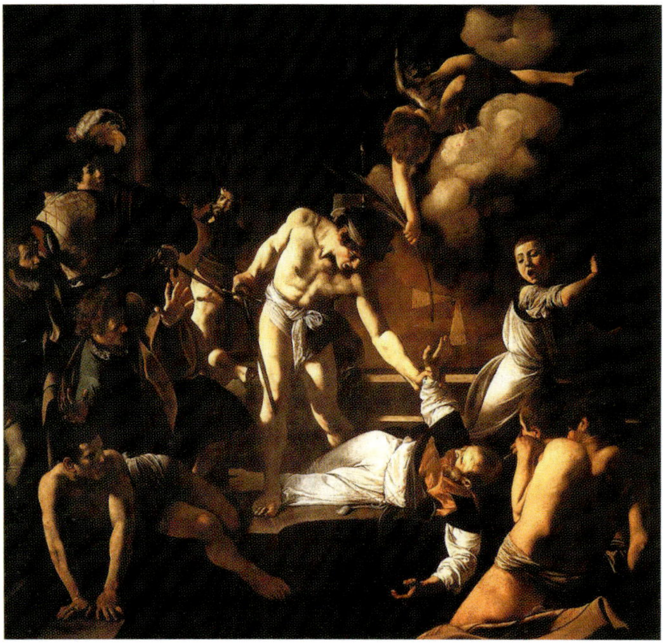

The work which best represents the combination of artistic influences originating from both is attributed to the Lombard Giuseppe Vermiglio (1587-1635) and represents *Cain and Abel*. Cain twists Abel's hand while wielding his club against his vanquished brother.[11] Abel struggles underneath the pressure of Cain's left foot; the main action happening in the painting is linked to the landscape in the background where Abel's sacrifice to God is identified as the reason for the fratricide. The painting belonged to the Grand Master's Palace collection and could have been acquired during the Magistracy of Grand Master Alof de Wignacourt. Indeed Vermiglio's painting might suggest an interesting remark on the violence then leading to brawls and fights among the often unruly knights in Malta.

Scholars have commented on the interesting similarities between this work and other versions of the same subject by Vermiglio. The painting relates in style to Vermiglio's *Doubting Thomas* being the only secure painting by the artist's hand and dateable to 1612 (church of San Tommaso in Vincis, Rome) This is essentially a Caravaggesque painting in both concept and style. Vermiglio was born in northern Italy and is documented as active in Rome between 1604 and

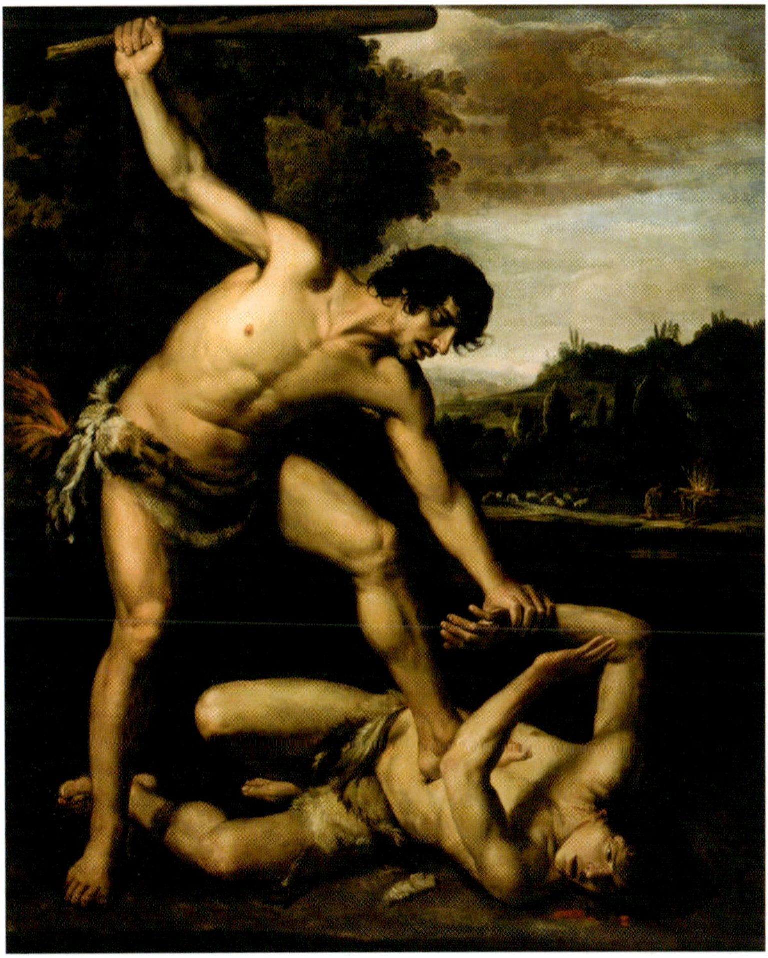

Giuseppe Vermiglio, ***Abel and Cain***, Valletta, National Museum of Fine Arts

1619. He left Rome for Lombardy and Piedmont slightly later where his works became more indebted to the Bolognese school of Annibale Carracci and Guido Reni. Vermiglio's *Cain and Abel* draws directly from Caravaggio's *Martyrdom of St Matthew* (Contarelli Chapel, San Luigi dei Francesi, Rome) but combines this caravaggesque influence with stylistic elements derived directly from Carracci. The combination of elements derived from Caravaggio, Reni and Carracci suggest a date in the second decade of the 17th century for Vermiglio's painting.

Caravaggio's influence on the generation of artists that followed is indeed multifaceted. Many explored the artist's style for brief tracts of time later opting to go for idealisations. Some would combine the ideal with the careful observation of nature whilst others would develop his style through devices in composition and subject matter that places their work closer to that of Caravaggio. Indeed, his art had an important impact which cannot go unrecognised. The works of the followers of Caravaggio in our national collection indeed represent a wide spectrum of artistic activity influenced by the style of this great master. The patronage of Caravaggesque paintings and the interest by connoisseurs in his followers was instrumental in building such a representative collection.

Grand Master Alof de Wignacourt - timeline

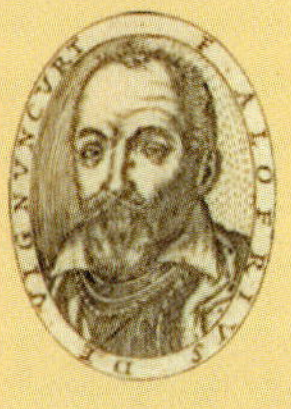

10 February 1601
Knight Alof de Wignacourt aged 54, Grand Infirmarian and Head of the Langue of France, is elected as the 11th Grand Master of the Order of St John in Malta

March 1602
Formal petition to the Order's Council for the building of the Oratory of the former Conventual church of St John's, today's Co-Cathedral

Februrary 1604
Chapter General of the Order held in Malta. It was decided to compile the laws and statutes of the Order into one volume for eventual publication.

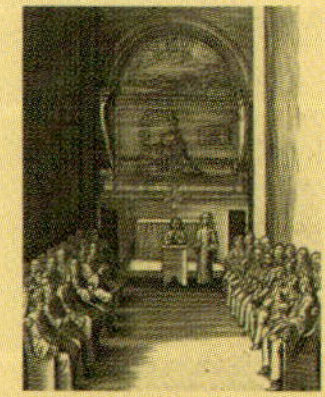

May 1604
The Order's fleet together with the Fleet of the Viceroy of Naples attacks the island of Lango (Aegean Sea), a former possession of the Order of St John

June 1607
Foundation of the Monte della Redenzione degli Schiavi. In March 1618, the noble lady Caterina Vitale known as *La Spetiala* was to bequeath tracts of land in Selmun to this foundation through her will.

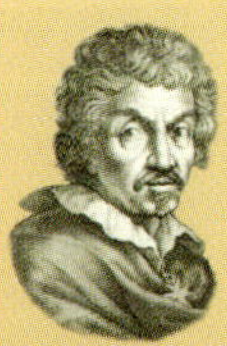

July 1607
Caravaggio arrives in Malta

The Order's Counci deliberates the construction of Fort St Lucian at Marsxlokk. The fort was completed a few months later at cost of 11,745 *scud*

The Order's fleet attacks Laiazzo (Yumurtalik, Turke

Beatification of St Ignatius of Loyola, founder of the Jesuits. The Jesuit church in Valletta i completed.

January 1610
The Order's Counc deliberates the building of an aqueduct to bring water from Rabat t Valletta. at the cos of 114,868 *scudi*.

1601 — *1605* — *1610*

August 1602
The Order's fleet attacks the city of Mahometta (Hammamet - Tunisia)

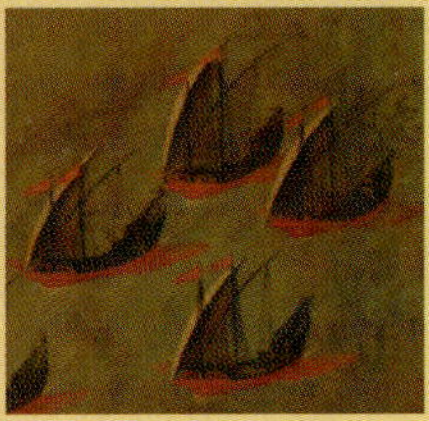

April 1603
The Order's fleet attacks the cities of Lepanto (Nafpaktos, Greece) and Patras (Patras, Greece)

Corsairing is regulated through the newly founded the Magistero degli Armamenti

April 1606
Shipwreck of three galleys including the *Capitana*. The lost galleys were replaced within a few months

September 1607
Wignacourt visits Gozo

October 1608
The local authorities realize that Caravaggio had escaped from Malta

February 1610
Laying of the first stone of a fort in St Paul's Bay to be completed within a year. The cost of this fort totalling 6,748 *scudi* was paid for by Grand Master Wignacourt in his personal capacity.

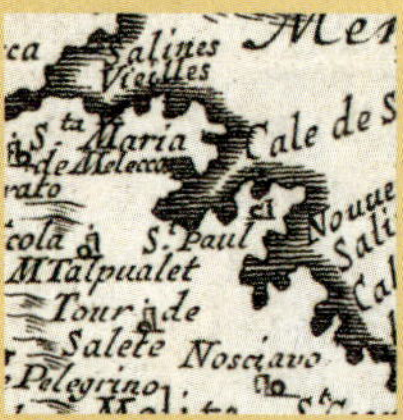

The Order's Fleet attacks Corinth (Greece

Failed attack by the Order's Galleys Navarin (Greece

Source: Hannibal P. Scicluna, 1925

June 1614
Death of the Bishop Tommaso Gargallo (1578-1614). He was interred in the Jesuit church.

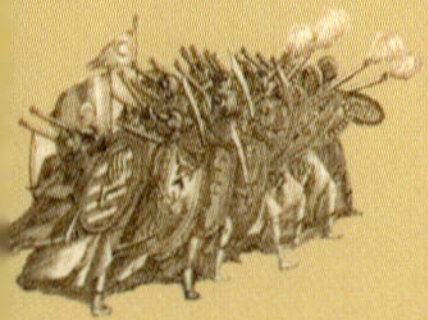

August 1614
Laying of the first stone of St Thomas Tower in Marsascala to be completed a few months later at a cost of 10,450 *scudi* paid by Grand Master Wignacourt.

July 1614
52 Ottoman galleys attack Malta. They manage to land in St Thomas bay and proceed towards Zejtun pillaging the countryside and its rural settlements. The Ottomans are pushed back by a heavy counter-attack.

August 1615
Death of Wignacourt's brother, Jacques de Wignacourt, at Verdala Castle, buried in the Chapel of France in the Conventual church of St John.

April 1617
The Order of St John takes over St Paul's Grotto in Rabat. The donation was made possible thanks to a papal bull granted by Pope Paul V to the then procurator of the Grotto, the Spanish hermit Juan Benegas de Cordoba. A college is founded by Wignacourt soon afterwards.

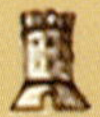

Laying of the first stone of a fort on the island of Comino. The cost was to total 18,628 *scudi*.

The Order's Fleet attacks the Castel Tornese in Morea (Hlemoutsi - Greece)

Building of the Fort of Our Lady of Graces in the vicinities of Zabbar

The Bali de Bellay, a relative of Grand Master Wignacourt builds the original chapel of Our Lady of Liesse.

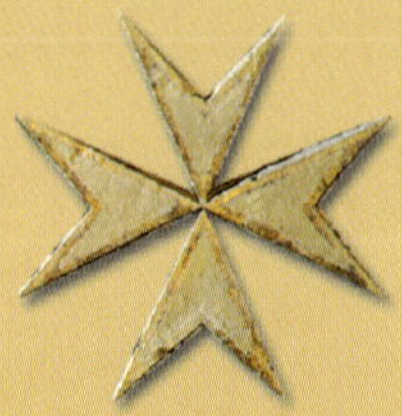

1615

Wignacourt calls a second General Chapter of the Order of St John.

Building of the original chapel of the Langue of Castille and Portugal dedicated to St James the Less, patron saint of Spain. The chapel was rebuilt in the 18th century to the designs of architect Romano Carapecchia (1668-1738).

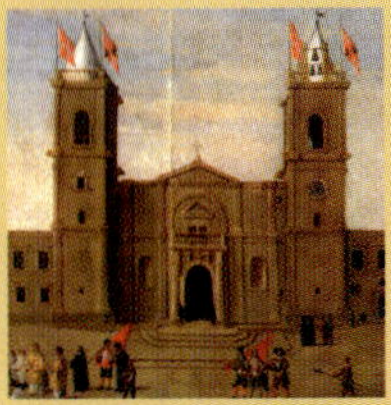

21 April 1615
Water arriving in Valletta through the newly built aqueduct sprouts for the first time from the fountain constructed in front of the Grand Master's palace. The aqueduct had taken 600 workers four years to complete. The Neptune's Fountain at Marina Wharf is built shortly afterwards.

May 1615
The Conventual chaplain of the Order of St John Balthasarre Cagliares (1615-35) is chosen Bishop of Malta.

1620

Commendator Giorgio Nibbia builds a chapel with an adjoining cemetery in the vicinities of the *Sacra Infermeria.*

14 September
Death of Grand Master Alof e Wignacourt aged 75. He had been taken ill a few weeks before after suffering from sunstroke during a hunting spree. He is interred in the crypt of St John's Co-Cathedral.

SELECT BIBLIOGRAPHY: 'A MAN CALLED CARAVAGGIO'

John Azzopardi, 'Caravaggio in Malta: An Unpublished Document' in *The Church of St John in Valletta, 1578-1978*, Malta, 1978

Antonio Ernesto Denunzio, 'New Data and Some Hypotheses on Caravaggio's Stay in Naples' in *Caravaggio – The Final Years*, Naples, 2005

Walter Friendlander, *Caravaggio Studies*, Princepton University Press, 1974

Helen Langdon, *Caravaggio – A Life*, London, 1999

Roberto Longhi, *Caravaggio*, Editori Riuniti, 1968

Keith Sciberras, 'Frater Michelangelus in Tumultu: the cause of Caravaggio's imprisonment in Malta', *The Burlington Magazine* vol. CXLIV no.1189 [April 2002]

Keith Sciberras, David Stone, *Caravaggio, Art, Knighthood, and Malta*, Midsea Books, Malta, 2006

Vittorio Sgarbi, *Caravaggio*, Milan, 2007

NOTES TO 'CARAVAGGIO'S MALTA'

1 Antonio Ernesto Denunzio, 'New Data and Some Hypotheses on Caravaggio's Stay in Naples' in *Caravaggio, The Final Years*, Electa, Naples, 2005. The author however quotes two galleys.

2 For a brief, yet detailed reference to Wignacourt's magistracy see Hannibal P. Scicluna, *Il Gran Maestro Alof de Wignacourt Attraverso un Manuscritto*, Malta, 1925.

3 Roger Degiorgio, *A City by an Order*, Malta, 2005, 175.

4 Thomas Freller, 'Malta Africana or Malta Europea' in Nicholas De Piro, Vickyann Cremona (Eds.), *Costume in Malta*, Fondazzjoni Patrimonju Malti, 1998, 41.

5 Sandro Debono, 'La Valette's Sword and Dagger – A Sixteenth Century Spanish Homage for Valor and Courage' in *The Sword of Valour*, Fundacion Jaume II El Just, Valencia, 2006.

6 See Carmel Cassar, *Society Culture and Identity in Early Modern Malta*, Mireva, Malta, 2002.

7 See Thomas Freller, 'Visitors Describe Treasures in Malta (1530-1630)' in *Treasures of Malta*, Vol. 3, No. 3, Fondazzjoni Patrimonju Malti, 1997.

8 For a detailed description of this entourage and a brief overview of Caravaggio's acquaintances in Malta, see K. Sciberras and D. Stone, *Caravaggio, Art, Knighthood, and Malta*, Midsea Books, Valletta, 2006, 24-25.

9 Joseph C. Sammut, 'Coinage in Malta' in *Treasures of Malta*, No. 35, Easter 2006, 38.

10 See Cassar, 2002. A significant wage increase for both is only noted 40 years later.

11 See Philip Farrugia Randon, *Caravaggio Knight of Malta*, AVC Publishers, Malta, 2004.

12 See Giovanni Bonello, 'Freedom of Expression under the Grand Masters' in *Histories of Malta – Reflections and Rejections*, Fondazzjoni Patrimonju Malti, Vol. 5, 29.

13 John Azzopardi, 'Caravaggio in Malta: An Unpublished Document' in *The Church of St John in Valletta, 1578-1978*, Malta, 1978.

14 Archives of the Order of Malta, Vol. 6128, fol. 19 onwards. Marchese's palace in Messina was located opposite Porta Cannizzaro. The 1628 reference also mentions the Prior of Messina Fra Nicolò della Marra and the Commendatore Giulio Accarigi.

15 For a history of the Carmelites in Valletta see Laurence Sammut, *Is-Santwarju tal-Karmnu*, Progress Press, Malta, 1952. For a history of the Dominican Community in Valletta see M. Fsadni, *Id-Dumnikani fil-Belt, 1569-1619*, Veritas Press, 1971.

16 See F. Azzopardi, 'The Veneration of the Blessed Virgin Mary in the Franciscan Capuchin Churches During the XVIIth and XVIIIth Centuries', in V. Borg (Ed.), *Marian Devotions in the Island of St Paul*, The Historical Society, Malta, 1983.

17 For a history of the Discalced Carmelites see Angelicus Busuttil, 'The Discalced Carmelites – A new Marian Order in 17th century Malta', in V. Borg (Ed.), Malta, 1983.

18 For a brief biography of the Knight Pietro Gonzalez de Mendoza see S. Debono, 'Kwadru u Grajja – Il-Kwadru tal-Artal ta' San Girgor fil-Knisja Parrokkjali l-Qadima ta' Santa Katarina' *(Zejtun)*, Malta 2002.

19 Giovanni Bonello, 'Fra Giorgio Nibbia and the Church that Vanished' in *Histories of Malta, Reflections and Rejections*, Vol. 5, 134-146.

20 Sandro Debono, 'Ancient and Modern Malta, Siculo-Maltese links and the Grand Tour', forthcoming.

21 Joseph F. Grima, 'Galley Replacements in the Order's Squadron c.1600-c.1650' in *Melita Historica*, Malta Historical Society, 1980, 48-60.

22 On the armoury and military activity in Malta see Stephen Spiteri, *The Palace Armoury – A*

Study of a Military Storehouse of the Knights of the Order of St John, the author, Malta, 1999.

23 Giovanni Bonello, 'Bontadino de Bontadini, The Murder of the First Baroque Architect in Malta' in *Histories of Malta, Convictions and Conjectures*, Fondazzjoni Patrimonju Malti, Malta, Vol. IV, 2003, 44.

24 See Stephen Spiteri, 1999.

25 Giovanni Bonello, 'Caravaggio, Friends and Victims in Malta', *Histories of Malta, Ventures and Adventures*, Fondazzjoni Patrimonju Malti, 2005.

26 See Table 5 in Cassar, 2002, 75.

27 John Azzopardi, 'Juan Benegas de Cordoba; l'Eremita che Trasferi la Grotta di San Paolo' in J. Azzopardi (Ed.), *The Cult of St Paul in the Christian Churches and the Maltese Tradition*, Malta, 2005.

28 See Alberto Guglielmotti, *La Squadra permanente della Marina Romana, Storia dal 1573 al 1644*, Rome, 1882.

NOTES TO 'IMAGES OF THE DIVINE'

1 For a general overview of the contents referring to works of art cited in this paper see Antonio Espinosa Rodriguez, *Paintings at the National Museum of Fine Arts*, Said International, Malta, 1990; Dominic Cutajar, *Museum of Fine Arts Valletta, Malta – A Commentary on its History and Selected Works*, Museums Department, Malta, 1991. References to paintings in the Palace collection (Malta) are mainly taken from Blanch Linntorn Simmons, *Description of the Governor's Palaces in Malta*, 1895.

2 Various authors, *Museum Guide Book*, Real Academia de San Fernando, Madrid, 2004.

3 Various authors, *Dopo Caravaggio, Bartolomeo Manfredi e La Manfredania Methodus*, Arnaldo Mondadori Editore, 1987.

4 Marina Mojana, *Valentin de Boulogne*, Eikonos Edizioni, 1989.

5 Liesbeth M. Helmus, 'Il Carattere Olandese di Utrecht' in *Caravaggio e l'Europa; Il Movimento Caravaggesco Internazionale da Caravaggio a Mattia Preti*, (Exhibition Catalogue), Milan, 2005.

6 Benedict Nicolson, 'Stomer Brought Up-To-Date' in *The Burlington Magazine*, April 1977, 230-244.

7 See *The Museum Bullettin*, Vol. 1, No. 1, 1929.

8 Antonio Espinosa Rodriguez, *The Paintings at the Cathedral Museum, Mdina*, Progress Press, 2005, 77.

9 M. Natale, *Museo Poldi Pezzoli – Dipinti*, Milano 1982, cat. 211, p. 163; N. Spinosa, *Ribera. L'opera completa*, Naples 2003, 320.

10 Clovis Whitfield and Jane Martineau (Eds.), *Painting in Naples from Caravaggio to Giordano*, (Exhibition Catalogue), Royal Academy of Arts, London, 1982.

11 See John Gash, 'The Cain and Abel in the National Museum: the Case of Giuseppe Vermiglio' in *Melita Historica*, Malta, 1998, 267-280.

BIBLIOGRAPHY

Primary Sources

Archives of the Order of Malta, Vol. 6128

Published Sources

John Azzopardi, 'Caravaggio in Malta: An Unpublished Document' in *The Church of St John in Valletta, 1578-1978*, Malta, 1978

John Azzopardi, 'Juan Benegas de Cordoba; l'Eremita che Trasferi la Grotta di San Paolo' in J. Azzopardi (Ed.), *The Cult of St Paul in the Christian Churches and the Maltese Tradition*, Wignacourt Museum, Rabat, 2005

Giovanni Bonello, 'Bontadino de Bontadini, The Murder of the First Baroque Architect' in Malta', *Histories of Malta, Convictions and Conjectures*, Vol. IV, 2003

Giovanni Bonello, 'Fra Giorgio Nibbia and the Church that Vanished' in *Histories of Malta – Reflections and Rejections*, Fondazzjoni Patrimonju Malti, 2004

Giovanni Bonello, 'Freedom of Expression under the Grand Masters' in *Histories of Malta – Reflections and Rejections*, Fondazzjoni Patrimonju Malti, 2004

Giovanni Bonello, 'Caravaggio, Friends and Victims in Malta', *Histories of Malta, Ventures and Adventures*, Fondazzjoni Patrimonju Malti, 2005

Vincent Borg (Ed.), *Marian Devotions in the Island of St Paul*, The Historical Society, Malta, 1983
Caravaggio-The Final Years, Exhibition Catalogue, Electa, Naples, 2005
Carmel Cassar, *Society Culture and Identity in Early Modern Malta*, Mireva, Malta, 2002
Dominic Cutajar, *Museum of Fine Arts Valletta, Malta – A Commentary on its History and Selected Works*, Museums Department, Malta, 1991
Sandro Debono, 'Kwadru u Grajja - Il-Kwadru tal-Artal ta' San Girgor fil-Knisja Parrokkjali l-Qadima ta' Santa Katarina' (Zejtun), Malta 2002
Sandro Debono, 'La Valette's Sword and Dagger – A Sixteenth Century Spanish Homage for Valor and Courage' in *The Sword of Valour*, Fundacion Jaume II El Just, Valencia, 2006
Sandro Debono, 'Ancient and Modern Malta, Siculo-Maltese links and the Grand Tour', 2007, forthcoming
Roger Degiorgio, *A City by an Order*, Progress Press, Malta, 2005
Dopo Caravaggio, Bartolomeo Manfredi e La Manfrediana Methodus, Exhibition Catalogue, Arnaldo Mondadori Editore, 1987
Thomas Freller, 'Visitors Describe Treasures in Malta (1530-1630)' in *Treasures of Malta*, Vol. 3, No. 3, Fondazzjoni Patrimonju Malti, 1997
Thomas Freller, 'Malta Africana or Malta Europea' in Nicholas De Piro, Vickyann Cremona (Eds.), *Costume in Malta*, Fondazzjoni Patrimonju Malti, 1998
Walter Friendlander, *Caravaggio Studies*, Princepton University Press, 1974
Mikiel Fsadni, *Id-Dumnikani fil-Belt, 1569-1619*, Veritas Press, Malta, 1971
John Gash, 'The Cain and Abel in the National Museum; the Case of Guiseppe Vermiglio' in *Melita Historica*, Malta Historical Society, 1998
Joseph F. Grima, 'Galley Replacements in the Order's Squadron c.1600-c.1650' in *Melita Historica*, Malta Historical Society, 1980
Alberto Guglielmotti, *La Squadra permanente della Marina Romana, Storia dal 1573 al 1644*, Rome, 188Liesbeth M. Helmus, 'Il Carattere Olandese di Utrecht' in *Caravaggio e l'Europa; Il Movimento Caravaggeso Internazionale da Caravaggio a Mattia Preti*, (Exhibition Catalogue) Skira Editore, 2005.
Helen Langdon, *Caravaggio – A Life*, London, 1999
Blanch Linntorn Simmons, *Description of the Governor's Palaces in Malta*, 1895
Roberto Longhi, *Caravaggio*, Editori Riuniti, 1968
Marina Mojana, *Valentin de Boulogne*, Eikonos Edizioni, 1989
The Museum Bullettin, Vol. 1, No. 1, 1929
Museum Guide Book, Real Academia de San Fernando, Madrid, 2004
Mauro Natale, *Museo Poldi Pezzoli – Dipinti*, Milano, 1982
Benedict Nicolson, 'Stomer Brought Up-To-Date' in *The Burlington Magazine*, April 1977
Philip Farrugia Randon, *Caravaggio Knight of Malta*, AVC Publishers, Malta, 2004
Antonio Espinosa Rodriguez, *Paintings at the National Museum of Fine Arts*, Said International, Malta, 1990
Antonio Espinosa Rodriguez, *The Paintings at the Cathedral Museum, Mdina*, Progress Press, 2005
Joseph C. Sammut, 'Coinage in Malta' in *Treasures of Malta*, no. 35, Easter 2006
Lawrence Sammut, *Is-Santwarju tal-Karmnu*, Progress Press, Malta, 1952
Keith Sciberras, 'Frater Michelangelus in tumultu': the cause of Caravaggio's imprisonment in Malta' in *The Burlington Magazine*, Vol. CXLIV, No.1189, April 2002
Keith Sciberras and David Stone, *Caravaggio, Knighthood, and Malta*, Midsea Books, Valletta, 2006
Hannibal P. Scicluna, *Il Gran Maestro Alof de Wignacourt Attraverso un Manuscritto*, Malta, 1925
Vittorio Sgarbi, *Caravaggio*, Skira Editore, 2007
Nicola Spinosa, *Ribera. L'opera completa*, Naples 2003
Stephen Spiteri, *The Palace Armoury – A Study of a Military Storehouse of the Knights of the Order of St John*, Malta, 1999
Clovis Whitfield and Jane Martineau (Eds.), *Painting in Naples from Caravaggio to Giordano*, (Exhibition Catalogue), Royal Academy of Arts, London, 1982